THE BOOK ON
NONPROFITS

Lessons Learned on
My 30 Year Journey of
Service to Others

SCOTT W BROWN

MOTIVATE AND INSPIRE OTHERS!
"Share This Book"

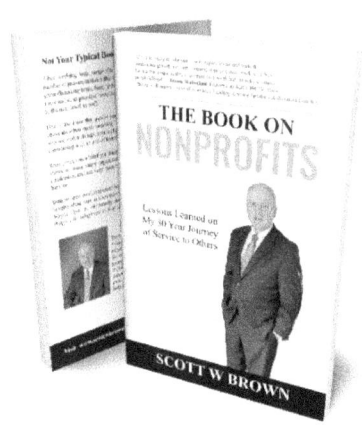

Retail $16.95

Special Quantity Discount

5 – 20 Books	$15.95
21 – 99 Books	$14.95
100 – 499 Books	$12.95
500 – 999 Books	$10.95
1,000 + Books	$ 9.95

To Place an Order Contact:

scottb@scottwbrown.com

(914) 443-1298

THE IDEAL PROFESSIONAL SPEAKER FOR YOUR NEXT EVENT!

Any organization that wants to develop their people to become "extraordinary,"
needs to hire Scott W Brown for
a keynote and/or workshop training!

TO CONTACT OR BOOK
SCOTT W BROWN
TO SPEAK:

scottb@scottwbrown.com
(914) 443-1298

THE IDEAL CONSULTANT FOR YOU!

If you're ready to overcome challenges, have major breakthroughs and achieve higher levels, then you will love having Scott W Brown as your consultant!

TO CONTACT
SCOTT W BROWN:

scottb@scottwbrown.com
(914) 443-1298

Dedication

This book is dedicated to nonprofits all over the world whose commitment, caring, and service to others help to ease the burdens of those they serve and make the world a better place for us all.

"Your perspective is either your prison or your power."

Unknown

TABLE OF CONTENTS

INTRODUCTION 1

METHOD 7

When You Change the Way You Look at Things.....9

K.I.S.S. 22

APPLICATION 35

Change – Inevitable & Unavoidable 37

You Can't Give What You Don't Have 48

Service – It's a Matter of the Heart 63

What? How? Why? Who? 77

Who Do You Serve? 85

Leadership – It's Probably Not What You Think ...96

Communication – A Lost Art 106

Comfort Kills 120

The Power of Questions 133

SUMMARY 143

ACKNOWLEDGEMENTS 149

ABOUT THE AUTHOR 151

INTRODUCTION

Welcome to a very different book about nonprofits. When I initially did some research to see what was out there, I found hundreds of books addressing all the do's and don'ts of nonprofits - how to start a nonprofit, how to fundraise for a nonprofit, social media for nonprofits, how to manage a nonprofit, I even found "Nonprofits for Dummies." I also googled "nonprofits" and got over one billion hits, (1,600,000,000 to be exact) in a mere 0.58 seconds – many of those websites offering their own volumes of information and resources. The obvious conclusion – there's a ton of information out there about nonprofits.

Given the overwhelming abundance of information available to anybody and everybody interested in the world of nonprofits, my dilemma became obvious – what value can I add to the dialog? What can I say that hasn't already been said in a variety of different ways? The answer was simple – <u>my</u> story; lessons I've learned and insights I've been blessed to have gained during my over thirty years of service to others via nonprofits.

In the most basic terms a nonprofit, like any other organization, is simply a group of people that have come together (the organization) to work towards accomplishing a common goal or purpose (mission) – the key being "people."

As a result, what you're about to read will not address all the rules, regulations, policies, and procedures that govern most, if not all, nonprofits – that information is readily available at the drop of a Google search. Rather than address "what" nonprofits do and/or "how" they do it, this book will focus more on the "who" does the doing and "why" nonprofits do what they do – the people issues.

I suspect that some of what is contained in the following pages you may have already considered and possibly discarded – that's perfectly fine. What I would ask is that you reconsider. If ever a paradox held true it's, *"The only thing that never changes is that things always change"* – and often rapidly. Things that may not have been appropriate for your organization months ago, may be completely appropriate and fit nicely within your organizational framework today. Also, please do your best to be honest with yourself and consider why you may have discarded these ideas in the past. Was it because they just didn't fit into your organizational culture at the time? Were they not applicable to what you do? Or was something else in play – difficulty in implementation, personal biases, ego, issues with other people or organizations, etc.? Maybe it's time to rethink things, reassess what might work and what won't, maybe not, but I do hope that you'll always give an idea a second chance.

You may think some of what follows is ridiculous or absurd to even consider. Again, the question I hope you ask yourself is "Why?" It's amazing what can come out of what might seem ridiculous, absurd, or even impossible. Think of all the things we take for granted today that a mere one hundred years ago would not only have seemed absurd and impossible but could have gotten you ostracized from society for even mentioning – man landing on the moon, organ transplants, quantum physics, civil rights, etc. The list goes on and on but I think you get the point. What may have seemed ridiculous yesterday can have tremendous potential in the light of a new day. Oh, and sometimes... it is absurd and/or ridiculous... but don't give up on it, there's usually a nugget of value in there somewhere.

During my three-decades-plus career serving nonprofits one of the many areas I was responsible for was policy and procedure development – Employee Handbooks, Policy and Procedure

Manuals, etc., all useful in helping an organization run smoothly and efficiently. After decades of policy creation, I have come to realize that a good policy covers about 90% to 95% of the issues, 90% to 95% of the time. And so it is with this book.

There will always be an exception to the rule and you will always be able to find an example of something that falls outside the discussion on the ensuing pages... I get it. For me to cover all those exceptions this book probably would have been a few thousand pages long and I strongly doubt you'd be reading it now. Rather, please accept this humble little book as a gesture of caring and help. Take from it what you can and make it your own, whatever you can't use feel free to discard with my thanks for the consideration.

One final note. You will notice as you go through the chapters that certain ideas, certain concepts repeat themselves. Please know that it's not carelessness, or my being unaware. Some, actually most, of the concepts presented on the following pages warrant being repeated multiple times because they are so important and integral to the topics being discussed. Truth be told, one of the things I've struggled with most is the actual order of the chapters because they are so interconnected, which in turn can make them difficult to separate into discreet topics.

In the end, I thank you for who you are and what you do and if this little book helps you along your way, then all the better.

Here's to those who serve!

SCOTT W BROWN

Part I

METHOD

The following two chapters, *When You Change the Way You Look at Things...*, and *K.I.S.S.* begin a journey that will provide the foundational framework for what will be discussed throughout the balance of the book.

It is my sincerest hope that they provide the reader with a "lens" through which to view the thoughts and ideas put forth in the second part of the book.

What is important to note, and will become obvious as you proceed, is that the concepts in these first two chapters are universal in nature and can be applied to virtually any issue an organization may face, or circumstance it may find itself in.

Understandably, the vast majority of organizations that find themselves in less-than-desired circumstances are tired of theory and are looking for practical, pragmatic tools that they can use and use <u>now</u>. Throughout my thirty-plus years of serving nonprofits I have found that these incredibly simple yet effective tools fit the bill and cannot only help resolve issues and challenges but in best-case scenarios prevent them from ever occurring in the first place.

Finally, these ideas, concepts, tools, however you want to label them, may challenge you. Know that you are up to the challenge, and maybe more importantly worth the challenge. Allow yourself and the ideas time and a certain amount of grace while trying to grasp the implications they present.

You've got this!

CHAPTER 1

When You Change the Way You Look at Things...

Most people recognize the chapter title as the first half of a well-known quote from one of my mentors, Dr. Wayne Dyer, and I suspect that you can probably complete it: *"When you change the way you look at things... the things you look at change,"* or put another way, when you change the way you think about things... the things you think about change. You might choose to call it changing your perspective, or changing your mindset. Any way you look at it (no pun intended) the idea is the same – how you look at things, how you think about things, how you perceive things, or simply changing your mindset, can have a significant and profound impact on whatever issue is being considered.

At first glance, the idea may seem incredibly obvious and even simplistic, but I have seen this one idea produce considerable change time and time again during my thirty-plus-year career.

Unfortunately, it never ceases to amaze me how many of the organizations I've worked with rarely employ this simple idea. Why? Possibly because it seems too simple to be of any value; or maybe it's because it smacks of being too "new age-like"; or maybe it's because it sounds more personal than professional. The actual answer is... none of the above. The heartening news is that once organizations understand the significance of this simple idea and embrace it, the impact can be felt almost immediately by all concerned – those within the organization as well as those served outside the organization.

Read Dr. Dyer's quote one more time, *"When you change the way you look at things... the things you look at change."* Pretty simple, right? And it is that very simplicity that makes it so effective while providing a prophetic segue into the next chapter, *K.I.S.S.*, but more on that later.

For now, let's take a deeper dive into this simple but powerful idea.

We can all look back on our own lives and see where a situation we considered to be negative, in time, turned out to be positive. That heart-wrenching break-up from the person we thought we would be with forever turns out to be the very thing that leads us to our soulmate. The loss of the job we thought was made for us turns out to be a redirection to a much more rewarding opportunity, etc. In each case what we thought initially, changed.

Of course, this works in the opposite direction as well. Things we thought were blessings turn out to be quite the contrary – the dream job turns out to be a dreadful situation that causes a knot in our stomach every morning before we get up to head to work; the dream partner turns out to be a nightmare; the investment that couldn't miss winds up tanking and taking our hard-earned cash with it. As with any idea there are always two sides to every coin.

A question that typically arises at this point is a fair one: "Is it the circumstances that change our perspective, or is it our perspective that changes our circumstances?" The simple answer is a resounding "Yes."

In the first instance where circumstances drive our change in perspective, we allow external factors, things we have little to no control over, to determine the change in our perspective – for good or bad. We have relinquished the responsibility for our decision-making and allowed things beyond our control to make the decision for us. We become a victim, again, for good or bad, but a victim nonetheless.

Sadly, the negative aspect of this very idea turns out to be one of the biggest issues I've seen manifest within many of the organizations I've worked with – organizations allowing circumstances to drive their thinking and subsequent behavior (sometimes it may be necessary but not anywhere near as often as people would like to believe). Initially, it may not seem like all that negative a thing but in the process organizations become reactive, constantly "putting out fires", hoping that somehow, some way, things will work out the way they want (which oftentimes is not the case). Organizations become powerless and dependent on things changing that are beyond their control, constantly dealing with stress and anxiety, and usually having to lower expectations as a result.

Is there a better option? Absolutely! Be proactive. Take ownership and control. Allow your own thinking to drive the decision-making process, and in turn outcomes, in the direction of your choosing. An old adage provides incredible insight into this idea – an ounce of prevention is worth a pound of cure.

Regardless of which scenario you participate in the principle always holds true – when you change the way you look at things... the things you look at change.

Two words in this principle bear taking a closer look at, the first being the word "you." In a world that often seems to be spinning out of control and well beyond our ability to influence it, there is something comforting and empowering to be found in being able to apply a principle that "you" are in direct control of. Look at the principle again only this time with targeted emphasis: When **YOU** change the way **YOU** look at things, the things **YOU** look at change. The key here is **YOU**.

The point is that this principle is something **YOU** can apply both here and now. It doesn't require a Board resolution or Board approval; it doesn't require a committee or task force or working group; it doesn't even require your boss' approval unless, of course, you happen to be the boss. All it requires is you, and a willingness and desire to utilize it.

The second word we need to take a closer look at that will help with our understanding and implementation of this principle is the word "change." Without going too far down the rabbit hole about the neuroscience involved, it suffices at this point to understand two basic ideas about how your brain works.

First, your brain absolutely loves, and I mean loves, what is familiar; we find comfort in the familiar. This explains why habits are so hard to break, why people stay in bad relationships or stay at jobs they don't like. To the brain the known, even if it's negative, is better than the unknown surrounding change – as the old 16th-century proverb states, "Better the devil you know." Given that "change" by its very nature isn't familiar, and is considered by many to be one of the greatest fears humans experience, ranked right up there with death and public speaking, is it any wonder that when the idea of change is presented to your brain it goes into overdrive to try to prevent it?

The extraordinarily high ranking of change on the list of human fears also represents one of the greatest ironic paradoxes known to humankind.

Why? Because the only thing that NEVER changes is that EVERYTHING ALWAYS changes.

Here are just a few astonishing facts to consider. In the minute (60 seconds) it takes you to read this the earth will have traveled 1,111 miles around the sun (that's 1.6 million miles a day), the solar system will have traveled 8,167 miles around the Milky Way galaxy (that's 11,760,500 miles a day), and the Milky Way galaxy will have traveled 21,667 miles through the expanse of the universe (that's 31,200,000 miles a day). In one minute, there will be 278 new lives on the planet, and 110 that will pass away. On a more personal note, in one minute, 300,000,000 cells in our bodies will die and 100,000,000 new red blood cells will be created. In total, your body will replace approximately 330 billion cells every day.

We could fill the rest of this book with the things that are constantly changing all around us but the point is simple: everything is in a state of constant change. Of course, all of this begs the question: If everything is always changing, why are we so fearful of the inevitable? Good question.

The second idea concerning how your brain works is that it will always work to move you away from anything it perceives as painful. Since change is perceived as "painful" as a result of its being unfamiliar, your brain does whatever it can to stop it using the proverbial "stick" (of carrot or stick fame).

This is why, as we will see in the next chapter, keeping things simple and small is instrumental in helping change fly under the brain's "change radar."

Finally, there is one last idea to be considered regarding change. There is a well-known, albeit not warmly received, expression that seldom gets the credit it deserves. As a matter of fact most people consider it silly, ridiculous, and/or absurd – take your choice – and poke fun at it at the drop of a hat. The expression? *It is what it is.* Be honest, what was your first thought? Silly? Ridiculous? Absurd? All three? That's okay, I get it, but after applying the very principle we're currently discussing – *When you change the way you look at things, the things you look at change* – that silly, ridiculous, and/or absurd expression will hopefully take on a whole new meaning.

At first glance it may appear to be a sign of resignation, and subsequently an excuse not to do anything, or possibly a filler when you're not quite sure what to say, but there is a profoundness to it when you change the way you look at it.

What if instead of assigning meaning or value to any given event, we acknowledged that it is the observer that assigns the meaning or value to a given event – the implications of this idea are profound. Simply stated, if the observer changes the way they look at an event then the meaning or value of that event can change without any actual change in the event occurring. Let's consider a few examples.

In this first example, there are two, separate observers. Let's say you're standing in a prestigious art museum staring at a picture you think a grade school child could have painted. You keep looking at the painting wondering how on earth anyone was silly enough to think that such a painting belonged anywhere where people would see it let alone in an art museum. Standing there, shaking your head, someone comes up alongside you extolling the genius of the painting and going on and on about the existential significance of the work, the dynamic use of color, and the artist's ability to capture the angst of societal problems in a post-modern world.

You stand there dumb-struck thinking they couldn't pay you enough to take the painting off their hands while the person standing next to you is marveling at the fact that the museum got the painting at a ridiculously cheap price of only $2.2 million. What's different? The painting "is what it is" – some colored tempura paint on a ten-foot by fifteen-foot canvas. The difference is in the perspective of the two observers – how each one "looks" at it.

While the above example is theoretical, let's take a quick look at a real-life example of differences in perspective. How much would you pay for a single banana? Yep, one solitary piece of fruit? At $0.59 per pound, you're probably looking at about fifteen cents. How much would you pay for about one foot of duct tape? Doing some quick math – a 60-yard/180-foot roll of duct tape sells for about $7.95, which equals a little over four cents per foot. Adding the cost of the banana and duct tape together we come up with a total cost of about twenty cents.

Good so far? Okay, here it comes. An Italian artist named Maurizio Cattelan sold a banana duct taped to a wall, entitled "The Comedian", at Miami's Art Basel for.... drumroll please... $120,000! I kid you not, $120,000. Ready for something even more astonishing? He sold not one, not two, but three "editions" of the work, the third going for an even higher price of $150,000! That's $390,000 for three bananas and three pieces of duct tape totaling a whopping sixty <u>cents</u>. Think perspective matters?

Let's take one last look at a different kind of example, this time with only one observer – a rainy day. You are faced with a rainy day, what do you do? You can stand there, shaking your fist at the sky, upset that you won't be able to go outside and get the yard work done, or take the walk you wanted to take, or simply bemoaning the grayness, OR you can change the way you look at things and look at the rainy day in a more positive light. You can feel good that everything is getting a nature-provided shower, animals are getting their water supplies refilled, aquifers that supply the water to your home are being replenished, and that circumstances have provided you with a perfect opportunity to have a cup of tea and to curl up on the couch with that book you've been meaning to get to.

In both cases the rainy day "is what it is", a rainy day, the only difference is how you choose to "look" at it.

I could go on and on with examples of how perspective changes everything, and I'm sure you could come up with numerous examples of your own – how an event or happenstance that was originally thought to be negative turned out to be a blessing in disguise. The event "was what it was", but your thinking about it, how you perceived it, changed and in turn changed what was once a negative into a positive.

I can't tell you how many times I've witnessed this simple mindset shift, perspective change, looking at things differently, turn things completely around and create significant, lasting change in an organization.

In the end, the key to all of this is that you have to be willing to change the way you look at things and not be so invested in your organization's programmed way of looking at things that you turn a blind eye and deaf ear to the possibilities around you.

To quote William Shakespeare, *"There is nothing good or bad, but thinking makes it so,"* or how about Henry Ford, *"Whether you think you can or can't you're right,"* or Albert Einstein who once said, *"The world as we have created it is a process of our thinking. It cannot be changed without changing our thinking."* I could quote a lot more amazing people but I think you get the point. It's how we "look" at things, think about things, perceive things that can make a difference for the better, and almost always, without exception that means change.

CHAPTER 2

K.I.S.S.

No, not the typical "Keep It Simple, Stupid" but close – Keep It Simple (and) Small. As the title implies, a "simple" concept, yet one that seems to elude a lot of people and organizations. It is also at the heart of much of what is contained in the balance of this book.

As we did in the previous chapter, we'll want to take a deeper dive into two of the words that are integral to this principle to get at the heart of why it's so powerful and useful. Let's start with the first "S" in K.I.S.S. – simple.

The Oxford dictionary defines the word "simple" as: *"easily understood or done; presenting no difficulty."* To quote some people who would know – Leonardo DaVinci, *"Simplicity is the ultimate sophistication."* Walt Whitman described simplicity as, *"the glory of expression,"* and of course there's one of my all-time favorites from Albert Einstein, *"If you can't explain it simply, you don't understand it well enough."* Regardless of your view, there is no denying that as a general rule "simple" makes things considerably more feasible and easier to implement especially in the short term.

With all the benefits simplicity has to offer it may be difficult to understand our infatuation with the complex and why, way too often, we choose complexity over the simple. However, after some research and giving it some thought some of the reasons become clear.

To start with, there is the erroneous assumption that somehow complexity equates to value – the more complex something is the more valuable it is – and although that may be true sometimes, it is far from true all the time. We scoff at the idea that something simple, and often obvious, has any substantive value.

The truth is that in many ways the value of something (i.e. material goods, ideas, etc.) is derived from the ability to use it. Think about it, if I were to give you a million dollars but told you you could never do anything with it – you could never spend it, you could never invest it, you couldn't give it away or donate it, you couldn't <u>do</u>

anything with it – how valuable would it be? If I were to give you a $500,000 car with the caveat that you could never drive it, sell it, donate it, or even show it to anyone how valuable would it be?

This same concept holds true for more esoteric things such as knowledge and ideas. Both are useless until they are used, until we put them into motion and do something with them. Which brings us full circle to the "value" of complexity versus simplicity. If something is so complex you can't use it or its use is minimally effective, if you can't put it into practice to accomplish something, why would we think that it's more valuable than something simple that you cannot only use but use sooner rather than later? A hard question to answer and yet complexity often rules the day – things that make you go "Hmmm???"

I recently saw a short film clip of a woman interviewing a young man and she asked, "So what would you say the biggest deception was? What was the biggest lie you were ever told?" His reply? "It's not that simple." That's the lie – "It's not that simple." The truth is that more often than not it is that simple. In some cases we create complexity by over-thinking and over-analyzing things which can lead to a phenomenon known as "analysis paralysis." Simplicity, and the clarity that comes from it, can be achieved by stopping, taking a deep breath, and then choosing to change the way you are looking at the issue, choosing a different perspective... sound familiar?

Unfortunately, and more often than we would like to believe, complexity is a conscious and well-thought-out strategy, foisted upon an unsuspecting public by those having a vested interest in confusion. They deliberately make issues more complicated than necessary to foster submission and dependence. Case in point: according to taxfoundation.org the United States tax code, laws, and regulations are a staggering 10 million words. By comparison, Leo Tolstoy's epic novel *War and Peace* is a mere 587,300 words.

Granted some things by their very nature are complicated – brain surgery, rocket science, quantum physics, the implications of infinity – but as a rule, and the keyword is "rule," a good number of things we label as complicated, aren't. A friendly warning – beware of complexity.

Next, let's move on to the second "S" in K.I.S.S. – small. Typically, the idea of small is associated with words such as minor, trivial, unimportant, or insignificant. And although that may be true in some cases, it is most definitely not true in all cases. In fact, small can be both valuable and powerful. Consider for a moment what would you think is more valuable, a one-ton chunk of granite or a one-carat diamond? As far as power is concerned, let us not forget that the most destructive man-made force on the planet, the atomic bomb, starts by simply splitting one tiny atom. Let's take a closer look at a few more examples that I think will drive the point home.

Have you ever heard of a gentleman by the name of Edward Lorenz? If not don't be upset, you are probably in the majority.

Edward Lorenz (1917–2008) was an American mathematician and meteorologist who was instrumental in creating the theoretical foundations for climate and weather probability. He is probably best known as the founder of modern "chaos theory" which is concerned with the high sensitivity of dynamic systems, such as the weather, to initial conditions – where a small initial change can result in a much larger change further down the road. He initially used the metaphor of a seagull flapping its wings to create a storm but later settled on a more poetic metaphor of a butterfly flapping its wings and subsequently creating a hurricane. Today we know this phenomenon as the Butterfly Effect.

In the early 1960's Lorenz was using a relatively primitive computer by today's standards, to simulate weather patterns utilizing a variety of variables including things such as temperature, wind speed, barometric pressure, relative humidity, etc. Wanting to see some of his initial findings again, he re-ran the simulation a second time, starting halfway through the original simulation. The second time through, one of the variables, a figure of .506127 was rounded to .506 with everything else remaining exactly the same. The result? All the predictions of the first model completely changed – a small change in the initial conditions had led to a massive change in the outcome.

You may not be familiar with the significance of June 18, 1815, but it was a date that changed the very fabric of world history and it all pivoted on a very small object.

Though you may not be familiar with the date, I suspect that everyone has heard of one of the principal persons involved in the major event that occurred that day – Napoleon Bonaparte, Emperor of France. On that fateful day in June 1815, Napoleon's army met a combined army of the British and Prussians under the command of the Duke of Wellington near the small, unassuming village of Waterloo, just south of the city of Brussels in present-day Belgium.

Without going into a lot of detail and risk boring you, one of the critical factors in the infamous Battle of Waterloo was a battery of 156 British cannons (artillery) that was wreaking havoc on the French positions. After the French cavalry had successfully overrun the British artillery, they were in the process of turning the newly captured cannon on their retreating enemy when the British regrouped and counter-attacked, recapturing the coveted artillery. In those days it was standard procedure for soldiers, especially those manning artillery pieces, to carry headless nails and a hammer. When there was a threat of artillery being captured, soldiers would drive nails into the firing holes in the top of the cannon rendering them useless. As the French officer witnessed the coming counter-attack by the British he ordered his men to *"Spike the guns!"* – to drive nails into the firing holes so the British couldn't resume using the artillery. There was just one problem... not one French soldier had any nails.

The result was immediate. The British trained the recaptured artillery on the French with devastating accuracy, the French lost the Battle of Waterloo, and with it, the reign of Napoleon Bonaparte, Emperor of France, came to an end. Napoleon was sent into exile for the second time on the remote island of Saint Helena in the Atlantic where he died in 1821. All for the want of a nail.

———————————

Speaking of "want of a nail", there are numerous versions of a proverb, one of which appeared in Benjamin Franklin's *Poor Richard's Almanac* in 1758, entitled "For the Want of a Nail":

For the want of a nail, the shoe was lost,
For the want of a shoe, the horse was lost,
For the want of a horse, the rider was lost,
For the want of a rider, the battle was lost,
For the want of a battle the kingdom was lost,
And all for the want of a horseshoe nail.

Different types of nails but in both cases, everything turned on something small – a simple nail.

I'd like to offer one more example that's much more personal in nature and one that you'll probably be able to relate to more easily than an American mathematician's weather predictions or French military generals on the field of battle.

It was a late day in August, 1973 and my parents were taking me to LaGuardia Airport in New York City for a flight to Peoria, Illinois, and the beginning of my college days at Bradley University.

At the top of the driveway we stopped to get the mail. A among other things there was a nine-by-twelve-inch manila envelope addressed to me with a return address of the Department of the Army. I opened the envelope and there, inside was a certificate awarding me a four-year Army ROTC (Reserve Officers' Training Corps) scholarship. The implications were significant – four years of college completely paid for including tuition, room and board, books, fees, and a small monthly stipend for incidentals. Four years of college paid in full!

I know what you're thinking, there's no such thing as a "free ride" for four years of college... and you'd be right. The scholarship came with a required four-year commitment to the United States Army after which I was free to go wherever I pleased. Given that I had gone to a military school for high school (yes, of my own choosing) and had tried to get into the United States Air Force Academy (getting a nomination from both a U.S. Senator and a member of the U.S. House of Representatives, but not an appointment), a career in the military was right up my alley. There was only one problem, Bradley University didn't have Army ROTC.

I remember looking at my parents and asking "What do we do?" I mean after all, it was four years of college paid for in full. My parents replied with a sigh of resignation, "Just go to school (Bradley)."

The point? If that envelope had come one day earlier, one small, insignificant day earlier, there would have been a lot more discussion, I probably would have gone to one of the other schools I had been accepted to that had Army ROTC, I most likely would have become a career

Army officer and wound up who knows where, and would not be writing this book now. For the want of one small day in the mail, the trajectory of my entire life changed.

I'm sure you can come up with numerous examples of your own where the course of your life was irrevocably changed based on some small decision, or what seemed to be a minor answer to a simple question at the time. Where a flip of a coin or an unexpected delay significantly changed things. Like the man who decided to wear a new pair of shoes to work one morning, got a blister on his foot, stopped at a drug store to get some first aid materials, and wound up being late to work. The date he decided to wear his new shoes? September 11, 2001. His place of work? The 82nd floor of the World Trade Center.

The longest journey begins... with one step; How do you eat an elephant? One forkful at a time; How do you lose 30 pounds? The same way you put it on, a few ounces at a time. The truth is everything is made up of "small" – matter is made up of atoms, journeys are made up of steps, lives are made up of moments. The list goes on and on but I'm sure you get the point.

The whole idea of simple and small having a substantial impact and/or making things easier in the process has been around for as long as people have inhabited the planet which has always made me wonder why people don't embrace them more often.

Embrace the idea. Try it you'll like it! Remember, when you change the way you look at things... the things you look at change.

Part II

APPLICATION

Application is where the proverbial rubber meets the road. This is where "value" is determined, after all, how valuable is a tool if you can't use it, or even worse, you overcome your struggles to use it and it doesn't work?

During the decades I've spent working with nonprofits I have certainly seen more than my fair share of new ideas and theories come and go. Some were good in theory but difficult or inappropriate in application. Some were just abysmal from the start and made me wonder what people were thinking of and if they had ever been able to apply their ideas in their own organizations.

I am happy to report that when it comes to the two "methods" you just read about, I have not only witnessed them successfully employed by others but I have also used them throughout my career with amazing results.

The following chapters represent a mere sampling of areas and ideas where the methods previously discussed can be applied and how they can have a significant impact on any topic they are applied to.

Finally, as I mentioned in the introduction to the METHOD chapters, their application is universal. It is my hope that you don't limit their application to only those items addressed in the following chapters. Allow yourself to think "outside the box" and be prepared to enjoy the fruits of your courage when you choose to simply look at things differently... because when you do, the things you look at change.

Enjoy.

CHAPTER 3

Change – Inevitable & Unavoidable

We briefly touched on the idea of change in the first chapter, *When You Change the Way You Look at Things...*, but the idea of "change" is so integral to the overall message of this book that it not only warrants its own chapter but it also seems to be an appropriate place to begin our exploration of the concept of changing the way you look at things. Specifically, let's start with changing the way we look at the very idea of "change."

Previously, we discussed how your brain loves the familiar – pretty much the exact opposite of change – and how it perceives change as painful with the result that your brain does its very best to steer you away from changing, even if it's a good thing.

Before moving on it's important to note that contrary to what you may think your brain is not always your best friend and does not necessarily want what's best for you – that's not its job. Your brain's job, first and foremost, is to try and keep you safe – survival. It's not really interested in the aesthetics of a wonderful life, it's more concerned about your surviving to live a life.

Truth be told your brain is wired to be constantly on the lookout for things that could hurt you, for the negative – or at least what it perceives as something that could hurt you or is negative. Science has proven that something negative (i.e. a negative thought, a negative word, a negative action) is up to ten times more powerful, has ten times the effect, versus something positive. The reasoning is pretty simple to understand – the ramifications of ignoring something negative (the sabretooth tiger, the cliff's edge, the shady character, choose your own negative circumstance) have the potential of being much more severe and even life-threatening than ignoring something positive such as a kind word or a beautiful sunset.

Regardless of what any specific change may involve there are two overriding considerations that are extremely important to understand about change. The first is that it is inevitable, and the second is that it is unavoidable.

As we mentioned previously, change is occurring all around us, and even in us, every moment of every day, whether we're conscious of it or not. Most people will typically conceptualize change in terms of their own frame of reference and things that have the potential of having a direct impact on how they live their lives. Since many of these things (e.g. the new iPhone version, a new person at work, the demise of a favorite character on a television show, etc.) aren't inherently dangerous or critical to our well-being, it can be easy to rationalize change as "no big thing" and choose to ignore it, avoiding the unpleasantness of having to deal with it.

However, the problem with this often-time nonchalant attitude is that the magnitude of the change that is actually occurring, and its real-life implications to our very lives, is not readily comprehended by most people – a simple case of seeing what we want to see, and hearing what we want to hear. We can easily lull ourselves into a false sense of security by thinking that change may be occurring but not all that much, and even if it is occurring it doesn't really affect me personally so... The truth is you would be very, very wrong!

To begin to understand the magnitude of change that is taking place let's consider the following concept – "knowledge doubling." Knowledge doubling addresses the total volume of all human knowledge and estimates how long it would take that volume of knowledge to double in size. In 1900 it was estimated that knowledge doubled every one hundred years. In 1945 it was estimated that the knowledge base doubled every twenty-five years. By 2015 knowledge was doubling every twelve to thirteen months. As if that isn't scary enough, scientists at IBM estimate that due to the advances in technology, the internet and "internet of things," and artificial intelligence (AI), that soon the doubling of knowledge will occur every... twelve hours. Yes, you read that correctly, twelve <u>hours</u>.

To begin to grasp what that means in human terms, consider the following mental exercise involving the concept of doubling that asks the question: "Would you rather have one million dollars or a penny <u>doubled</u> every day for thirty days (i.e. on day one you start with one penny, on day two the amount increases to two pennies, on day three the amount goes up to four pennies, on day four the amount doubles to eight pennies, on day five the amount doubles to sixteen pennies, and so on for thirty days)?"

The typical, knee-jerk reaction by most is to take the million dollars and run. The unfortunate outcome of such a decision would be that you would wind up being $4,368,709.12 poorer than if you agreed to the penny doubling option – a penny doubled every day for thirty days would yield... $5,368,709.12. Imagine, you start with one single penny and at the end of thirty short days you would wind up with 536,870,912 pennies. Now apply that same concept to doubling knowledge not every day but every half day and you wind up with results that are all but impossible to comprehend.

Of course, a related question is, "How can human knowledge double so quickly?" The answer is simple, a bit scary, and alluded to by the IBM scientists on the previous page – prepare to have your mind blown.

When the first electronic programmable computer built in the United States (ENIAC) appeared in 1945, it could do lightning-fast calculations at a rate of 5,000 per second. Today, a mere seventy-eight years later, at the Department of Energy's Oak Ridge National Laboratory located in Oak Ridge, Tennessee, they have created a supercomputer (Frontier) that can do... one quintillion (that's 1 with eighteen zeros after it) calculations per second.

To put that into perspective, if every person on earth did one calculation per second, every second of every day it would take the entire planet's population over four years to do what this supercomputer can do in one second. If you're not feeling very community oriented and wanted to tackle the job by yourself it would only take you a mere 20-plus billion years. Think about it, what would take you over 20 billion years to do would only take this supercomputer one second. Mind blown?

It is this kind of exponential growth in the capabilities yielded by technology that is fueling knowledge doubling. In a word, technology is begetting technology and knowledge is the beneficiary.

So, what does this massive exponential explosion in both technology and the attendant human knowledge base have to do with you? If you consider the almost infinite applications such knowledge and technology would have in practically every field of human endeavor, it will be all but impossible for anyone on the face of the planet to not be affected by the changes that will inevitably occur.

So, there you have it, an argument that significant change is inevitable, unavoidable, and here to stay – now what?

Before going any further, I feel it necessary to make a few things clear. First, I am not advocating change for the sake of change. There are certainly some instances where, "If it isn't broken don't fix it," is as sound a strategy as any. However, there are also times when "If it isn't broken... you need to break it" is a more viable, and far better option. There will also be times when it may not be broken but whatever "it" is, isn't serving the organization well and needs to be discarded, retired, or upgraded.

Second, no organization has the resources, or more importantly the need, to address all the changes that will occur. Organizations need to be intentional, vigilant, and discerning regarding the identification of those changes applicable to them and their capabilities to address them, but I would encourage you to not be afraid to "think outside the box" when considering what changes you can take advantage of and what changes may affect those you serve.

There is also the issue of assessment. Organizations should consider developing policies, procedures, and processes that address the continual assessment and reassessment of the changing landscape around them. A change that may have been inappropriate to consider six months ago may now make complete and total sense to consider and implement... things change.

As with all things in life, there are options, choices to be made, however, in this instance there are really only two. Ironically, "not choosing" is a choice (i.e. choosing not to choose) – an extension of which would be to simply ignore change if at all possible. If the change can't be ignored, then fight it every step of the way with every tool in our toolbox. Unfortunately, in my thirty-plus years I've seen way too many organizations choose this path... initially.

They rationalize their recalcitrance with platitudes such as: honoring their roots, holding fast to the very things that the organization was built upon, loyalty to those things that have served them well in the past, the ever-popular "we've always done it that way," and "it doesn't resonate with our culture," among others. In the end, these excuses used to feel better about avoiding necessary change are just that, excuses.

If, after a while, an organization is able to work through and overcome the biases that do their best to maintain the status quo, they can shift things into an even higher gear, becoming more adept at coming up with rationale and pragmatic excuses for avoiding change. Typically, these will revolve around some perceived shortage of what they think are necessary resources – not having enough of the appropriate funding, not having the right people in place, etc. Again, reasons why they can't instead of how they can. It reminds me of that famous quote from Henry Ford, "Whether you think you can or think you can't, you're right."

There is an entire chapter (Chapter 10) dedicated to the idea of "comfort" but for now, suffice it to say that comfort and rationalization frequently go hand-in-hand. This dynamic duo are often overriding, determining factors when faced with the possibility of change and if not handled quickly and correctly can kill an organization from the inside out.

The second option, which is really the only viable option, is to embrace change and use it to your advantage. Again, be discerning but keep in mind the larger motivating picture – all great human achievement has occurred as a result of, and on the other side of, change.

Change can offer your organization the opportunity for a refresh, to do some spring cleaning, and to look at things that have become too familiar, too routine, too comfortable – out with the antiquated that's not serving anyone well, and in with new opportunities.

Change can provide the impetus for long-overdue upgrades in policies, procedures, processes, and organizational thinking.

Change can offer opportunities for employees to upgrade relevant skill sets and make work not only more challenging but meaningful as well.

Change can provide a wide variety of opportunities for you to become more efficient and effective with those you serve.

In a word, change can breathe new life into a stagnate, struggling organization.

There will always be an initial reluctance to change – remember, the brain loves what's familiar – and change will bring challenges, but without exception, every single challenge will contain the seed of an opportunity to become a better organization... if you look for it.

In the end change can become the best friend an organization has if that organization chooses to step out of its comfort zone, embrace it, learn what it has to offer, and honor the process that accompanies it.

Remember that accepting the challenges that accompany change is a choice. It is my sincerest wish that you choose wisely.

CHAPTER 4

You Can't Give What You Don't Have

In all my years of working with nonprofits, I have never had anyone raise their hand when asked the question, "Who does NOT want to deliver their organization's mission with excellence?" In all honesty, can you imagine anyone having enough indifference with their organization's mission to stand up and say, "Yeah, excellence is way overrated. I'd much rather be associated with mediocre, run-of-the-mill, or good enough." Almost sounds like nails on a blackboard, doesn't it?

Who would ever argue that excellence is not only a good thing (okay, a great thing) but the gold standard that everyone should be striving for? The problem then appears to be an apparent disconnect between what people say and what people do. Unfortunately, this disconnect is by no means a new phenomenon, nor is it unique to nonprofits.

There is a reason why axioms such as "Talk is cheap," "Actions speak louder than words," and "What you do speaks so loudly I can't hear what you say," have stood the test of time... all too often they are true. So, what's the answer? How do we work on at least closing the gap between what's said and what's done?

One of the immutable laws of the universe is simply this: *"You can't give what you don't have."* This is true for people in general and organizations of any size and purpose. This is especially true for nonprofits given that their sole purpose for being is to give to others in one form or another whether it be some type of service, goods, or a quality-of-life experience.

I suspect that when most nonprofit folks read this they will immediately think about the services and/or goods they have to offer to others. As important as what you have to offer is relative to excellence, the issue has to start internally (i.e. within the organization), remember the immutable law of the universe – Y*ou can't give what you don't have.* Just like joy and happiness are "inside jobs," so, too, is what an organization needs to do to prepare to give those you serve your very best – in a word, excellence.

Richard Branson, founder of the Virgin Group, which today controls more than 400 companies in various fields of endeavor, has been quoted as saying, "Your customers don't come first. Your employees come first. If you take care of your employees, they'll take care of your customers." – the same idea holds true for nonprofits as well. Take care of those inside the organization and they will take care of those you serve outside the organization. Take excellent care of those inside your organization and they will take excellent care of those you serve outside the organization. In my over thirty years of working with nonprofits I have witnessed this phenomenon time and time again – the quality of service and goods provided by an organization is directly correlated and proportional to the quality of care given to its employees.

––––––––––––––––––

Initially, one might think that the internal "quality of care" I'm referring to deals specifically with salaries. Although salary is important, I would hazard a very educated guess that most people don't work in the nonprofit sector for the money. I don't think it would be too much of a stretch to say that most positions within a nonprofit could make substantially more in the for-profit world doing comparable work.

For the majority of people working in the world of nonprofits they are there because they believe in the greater good, in service to others, in something bigger than themselves. For a lot, what they do is more than just a job, it's a "calling," something an internal compass compels them to do.

So, the question is, if I'm not referring to salaries what am I referring to? There are a variety of things but let's start with probably the most obvious.

Mission / Purpose

Is it enough for the people in your organization to know what you do? Is it enough to have seen or heard your mission statement or maybe even have gotten a copy of it? Not really. Remember what we talked about at the beginning of this chapter – about talk being cheap, and actions speaking louder than words. In the end, a mission statement is just words, meaningless hyperbole unless those words are backed up with consistent, meaningful, effective action and feedback.

Do ALL employees understand the impact those mission-related words have? You might think so but my experience tells me that's probably not true. Have you sought out and shared testimonials about the effectiveness and impact of what you're doing? Have you shared weekly or monthly statistics on how effective your organization has been in delivering on its promise? Even more importantly, have you/can you attach lives and faces to those statistics?

As a VP/Director of Finance and Administration for many years, no one gets the importance of numbers more than I do, but one of the lessons I had to learn over and over again, and keep remembering, is that we don't serve numbers, we serve people.

Bottom line, do your employees understand how important what you do is and the impact they're making in the lives of those you serve? There's a significant difference between reports and numbers, and truly knowing in the deepest part of your soul that what you're doing is making a real and lasting difference in people's lives. What's the adage? Nobody cares about how much you know until they know how much you care. It may sound trite but there's a reason it's an adage that has stood the test of time – it's true.

Qualifications / Skills

This point may seem obvious but it's surprising how often it's overlooked. Taking care of an employee starts at the very beginning, with the hiring process. It is vital that employees are set up for success from their first day with the organization.

To this end, it is important to make sure that job announcements and corresponding job descriptions are not only up-to-date but are representative of the things the employee will actually be doing once hired. The point? Keep the use of the catch-all job description statement, "And related work as required," to a bare minimum. I've seen this job description "loop-hole" cause the ruination of more than one good employee.

It is often said that you should hire for character and train for skills. As a rule, I would agree, and if that works for your organization fine, but where skills are lacking or need an upgrade, be sure to make allowance for appropriate training, don't just give it lip service. An employee who doesn't have the necessary skills to do the job will quickly become frustrated, resentful, and unhappy, and those you serve will know it.

Meetings

Meetings can be the bane of any employee's existence. Always consider if another form of information exchange (i.e. phone call, email, etc.) is appropriate. If a meeting is warranted it is important to respect everyone's time. Invite only those employees who need to be present and do your best to make sure there is some form of agenda (written preferably) and stick to it. Sharing agendas beforehand allows attendees to prepare and not be blindsided and potentially embarrassed by unanticipated questions or comments.

Consider having internal "town hall"-type meetings where people from various departments and areas not only get to meet each other periodically, but they get to interact with each other. What tends to differentiate this type of gathering versus a typical staff meeting is that instead of simply going around the table and reporting, people get to interact, ask questions, offer suggestions and feedback, and see how they fit into the overall scheme of things. Even if your organization is relatively small you may think that you're promoting a family-type atmosphere where positive interaction is occurring regularly, but it's both amazing and scary to see how often the left hand doesn't know what the right hand is doing regardless of an organization's size.

Another type of meeting that may prove helpful is instead of "Exit Interviews" – when people leave and you find out what went wrong too late to prevent a problem from occurring and possibly keeping a good person from leaving, consider periodic "Stay Interviews" – an informal sit-down to touch base, find out what's going on and get feedback on what's working and what's not. It's always easier to address issues before they pick up a head of steam. It's also good to know what's working or needs to be reassessed for possible improvement. Minor course corrections are always easier to make than major overhauls. Whatever format you choose the key is to make people feel heard, valued, and engaged.

As irritating as meetings can be perceived, if used properly and judiciously, they can provide an invaluable venue that can help employees feel that they are truly cared about and understood. Remember, only 7% of all communication is verbal so getting cues that only meeting face-to-face can provide is critical.

Safety

Another element of care is safety. Do people throughout the organization feel safe? Not just physically safe, although that's important too, but emotionally safe as well. Is there a generally accepted atmosphere where mistakes/failures are not only tolerated but acknowledged as a sign that people are trying? Albert Einstein once said, "A person who never made a mistake never tried anything new."

This is <u>not</u> to say that you should encourage mistakes (i.e. "Hey, let's all go out and see how many mistakes we can make."), or that there won't be people who at times make mistakes through simple carelessness, but last time I checked all our pencils have erasers on them. The point is that it is important that everyone understand that mistakes/failures are an integral part of the process of learning and success. There's not a person who learned to walk without falling down a number of times. Even the great American inventor Thomas Edison, when asked how it felt to have failed ten thousand times trying to invent the lightbulb replied, "I didn't fail ten thousand times, I simply learned ten thousand ways how not to make a light bulb." History is replete with examples of astounding successes borne of abject failure. Learn from your mistakes/failures and move forward.

One last point about an organization's attitude towards mistakes/failure. When an organization has a low or even negligible tolerance towards "failure" people will often adopt an attitude of fear, afraid to make a mistake for fear of retribution either in the form of ridicule, embarrassment, a poor annual performance review, or even worse, losing their job. Under these circumstances employees will often retreat to the safety of their own strengths and a strong desire to cover their own backs, not willing to risk failure and the subsequent chastisement. As a result, things like out-of-the-box thinking, pushing comfort zones, and collaboration with resultant synergies are often forfeited. Remember "failure" is simply success in progress.

Another element of the safe issue (that will be addressed more thoroughly in the chapter on communication) is the idea of people being able to say what's on their minds (respectfully of course) and voice their concerns without fear of retribution. Is there an environment within your organization that facilitates open discussion and dialog? To be clear, I'm not talking about whistleblower protections or an annual performance review process that may afford employees an opportunity to provide feedback, although these are important, I'm talking about a day-to-day environment where meaningful, deep dialog can take place if and/or when needed. To quote Andy Stanley, "[People] who do not listen will eventually be surrounded by people who have nothing to say." Communication and feeling heard are critical and proportional to an employee's level of engagement and sense of being cared for.

Value

Another issue critical to our discussion of care is the idea of being valued. Do people feel valued as people not just as a means to an end (i.e. what they do to help the organization accomplish its mission)? A crucial component of being valued is being heard. As we just discussed, do employees feel that they can speak openly and honestly, and that, most importantly, what they have to say matters? You need to remember that your organization serves people – both externally AND internally. If you don't have an attitude of service to each other internally, how can you expect to display such an attitude with those you serve externally?

Health and Wellness

One of the more obvious ways to show genuine caring for people is to address issues concerning their health and wellness. Things like the physical work environment – lighting, air quality, temperature, noise abatement, ergonomic workspaces, appropriate seating, comfortable eating areas, office layout to facilitate collaboration, etc. are all worthy of consideration.

What about health benefits? Do you have a positive, well-thought-out, usable, health plan? I once worked with an organization that offered health insurance that had a huge deductible put on the employees in order for the organization to save money on the employer's portion of the premiums. The problem was that the deductibles were so high that employees balked at the thought of using the supposed benefit and so let health issues go unaddressed until absolutely necessary. Penny wise and pound foolish.

Do you offer flexible spending accounts? Does your health insurance offer a wellness plan, gym membership, etc.? All these little benefits can go a long way in showing people in your organization that you care about them.

Once, when one of the organizations I was working with was having budget-balancing issues, employees became very open and vocal about what steps they thought should be taken to get things in balance. One of their suggestions surprised me – they would much rather have taken a cut in salary than a reduction in health benefits. Typically, employees will make it clear that health insurance is a priority over salary. Have the discussion, it matters.

One last thing, when in doubt, create an employee-populated working group to address health insurance needs and policy renewals. Understanding that many times finances become an issue when determining what level of plan the organization adopts, employees can have input into the process, understand why the decision that's eventually made is made, and help convey the reasoning to their fellow employees. Again, being heard matters.

Acknowledgment and Empathy

On the less tangible side, are successes and hard work and effort acknowledged, or are those viewed as simply doing one's job? Recognizing effort lets people know that it was not only noticed but that it matters.

If you notice that people inside your organization are struggling, depressed, or angry, rather than judge them, do you reach out to them and try to find out why and how you can help? Maybe it's seeking them out at lunch to talk, or sending them a simple card that says "I'm here if you need me." Maybe it's a simple smile or a look that says "It's going to be okay." Maybe it's simply taking the time to exercise a little empathy, trying to understand, and putting yourself in their shoes. The truth is everybody has a story;

everybody has things they've been through or are going through – be quicker to have compassion than to judge. One of the side benefits? When people feel valued as people they tend to reciprocate (they treat others the way they would like to be treated).

Although I could probably write an entire book on the topic of "caring," I'd like to offer one last thought that at first may not sound completely appropriate to the matter at hand but can go a long way in creating that caring space we're looking for... don't take things so seriously. I know what you do is important but don't make the mistake of equating importance with seriousness. I remember when I was young I would occasionally get in trouble when answering my parents. What I would hear after offering what I thought was a completely reasonable response was, "It's not what you said but how you said it." The point? How we do things can be as important as what we're doing. Relax. Lighten up. Have fun and enjoy the journey, and don't keep it a secret - let people know that you're enjoying it.

Given that we spend about twenty-five percent of our lives at work (40 hours out of a 168-hour week), be honest who would you rather spend that time with, someone who's always serious, never smiles and can be downright hard to talk with, or someone who can laugh, express the joy in what they're doing, who smiles and always seems to have a kind word to offer? Exactly. So why not be the reason someone, including you, smiles today? It's free and the benefits are priceless.

Ultimately, the decision as to whether someone feels valued and in turn shares those feelings and values with others in terms of excellence is a choice, a choice each person in an organization will ultimately have to make for themselves.

In the end, the question is do you have your hand on the pulse of the people in your organization? Do they feel included and a part of the whole? Are they excited about what your organization is doing and accomplishing? Do they feel heard, valued, and understood? Do they feel cared about as "people" first and not just what they're able to grind out for the sake of the organization? Are they happy? Are they healthy? Bottom line, do they possess the excellence you want to be able to give to others? Because... you can't give what you don't have.

CHAPTER 5

Service – It's a Matter of the Heart

Typically, when we think of service we think of "customer service" offered by organizations we have purchased either goods or services from.

In the previous chapter, *You Can't Give What You Don't Have*, I quoted Richard Branson: (paraphrased) "Customers don't come first, employees come first. Take care of your employees and they'll take care of your customers." Given the sad state of the customer service functions within many organizations, I'm led to one of two conclusions: either there are a ton of companies/organizations out there that aren't taking very good care of their employees, or Richard Branson's quote may work well within his own organizations but it's not transferable to the organization population as a whole. From what

I've witnessed firsthand I've chosen to focus on option number one.

I'm sure we can all recount dozens, if not hundreds of tales about horrific customer service at the very hands of those who say they want our business – I myself have had a number in the weeks leading up to my writing this chapter (thank you one and all).

I have to confess to being more than a little stunned at how many organizations out there are still in business given how horrendous their customer service is, especially when you consider the statistics and overall costs associated with bad service. Granted this is a generality but the fact that good service has become the exception as opposed to the rule speaks volumes. What should be the norm today strikes us as extraordinary.

It turns out that as bad as the state of customer service affairs may be, this may actually wind up being good news for your organization. Good news? How on earth can this be good news? I'm glad you asked.

There's a timeless story about a shoe company that sends one of its salesmen to Africa to do some research and open up a new market for its footwear. A week after arriving the salesman calls up company headquarters to speak to his boss – "Sir, you're not going to believe this but this trip has been a total waste of time. I have traveled and looked everywhere and nobody here wears shoes." Dejected the salesman returned home. About a month later another high-level executive in the company sends another salesman to Africa, not knowing that one of their salesmen had already been sent there a month earlier. This time however, the salesman calls up the home office ecstatic at what he found – "Boss, send me everything we have in stock, nobody here wears shoes!"

The point of the story is probably obvious – perspective changes everything, and what at first may seem like a significant problem (nobody wearing shoes) can in fact become a tremendous opportunity (selling shoes to all the people not wearing any).

Think about how applicable this idea may be when it comes to your organization providing quality customer service. When there is a noticeable scarcity of quality service, and there is, any organization that is willing to step into the gap and offer what is lacking elsewhere will most certainly stand out and above others and in the process attract droves of supporters.

Intention

Now I understand that some will argue that why you're doing what you're doing and the level of service associated with it doesn't really matter as long as whatever needs to get done gets done. However, there is strong evidence to support the idea that why you do what you do is just as important, possibly even more important, than what you do. Following is an example I've used several times to make the point.

About thirty years ago I taught Sunday school to a very challenging group of youngsters – junior high and high schoolers. One year, after welcoming everybody back from summer break I offered the following statement to kick off the new year: "It's not good enough to do the right thing." Well, you can imagine the reaction from a bunch of teenagers who had "Do the right thing" drilled into them for the better part of their lives. After the initial shock had subsided, I continued, "You have to do the right thing... for the right reason." Slowly the anger and disdain over my initial comment transformed into looks of questioning and curiosity. To illustrate my point, I offered the following example:

SCENARIO ONE – A husband is sitting on the couch when his wife, coming home late from work, comes through the front door elated. Before the door has a chance to close, the wife blurts out, "You'll never guess what happened to me at work today." Barely turning his head to acknowledge his wife's presence and enthusiasm the husband asks, "What?" The wife replies, "I was named Manager of the Year! They (the company) are going to have an awards dinner in three weeks and I'm going to get an award in front of everybody! I just want to make sure you can go." Finally, without even turning down the volume on the television, and shifting his body to now face his wife with a less than enthusiastic expression, the husband replies, "Great, another work thing. You know how much I love going to your work things." After a few seconds pause, the husband continues, "Yeah, I'll go because you know if I don't I'll never hear the end of it. Besides, if I don't go I'll probably be the only husband not there and I'll be the object of their ridicule so…" Three weeks later the husband puts on his suit, shirt, and tie, and accompanies his wife to the awards dinner.

SCENARIO TWO - A husband is sitting on the couch when his wife, coming home late from work, comes through the front door elated. Before the door has a chance to close, the wife blurts out, "You'll never guess what happened to me at work today." Turning off the television, getting up, and coming around the couch to stand in front of his wife, the now enthusiastic husband asks, "What? What happened?" Now holding her husband's hands the wife replies, "I was named Manager of the Year! They are going to have an awards dinner in three weeks and I'm going to get an award in front of everybody! I just want to make sure you can go." The husband embraces his wife and with as much enthusiasm as his wife, says, "That's incredible! I am so proud of you! It's about time that company of yours realized just how amazing you are! Wild horses couldn't keep me from going!" Three weeks later the husband puts on his suit, shirt, and tie, and accompanies his wife to the awards dinner.

Making sure that everybody was clear about the two scenarios I asked the students the following questions: Which scenario do you think is "better"? More uplifting? Which scenario do you think is more honoring to the wife and made her feel more loved and valued? I had barely gotten the words out of my mouth when the students started blurting out, "The second one!" "Number two!" Clearly, they got it. But the follow-up questions were the ones that turned on the lights: "Why? Both husbands did the right thing, didn't they? They both put on their suits, shirt, and tie, and went to the awards dinner, didn't they? If doing the right thing is all that matters, and they both did the right thing, why is the second scenario so much better than the first?

Yep. They got it. Without exception, they all understood that the first husband did the right thing because he was selfish and only concerned about what others might think of him. In contrast, the second husband was selfless and showed love and caring for someone else (others), his wife. It became crystal clear – <u>why</u> they did what they did mattered.

I suspect that as we just went through the two scenarios again, you had the same reaction and came to the same conclusions they did – even though both husbands did the right thing, husband number one was a jerk, and husband number two wasn't. Be honest, if you had to choose one of the two husbands as a friend, which one would you choose? You see, <u>why</u> you do what you do matters.

With this in mind, never underestimate the power of intention. If your intent in serving others is for what <u>you</u> can get out of it – "If I serve them then I'll get _____ (fill in the blank)," then you may be doing the right thing, but for the wrong reason.

It may produce acceptable results in the short term but eventually it will catch up with you. I am amazed at how often I've seen people see through the guise and understand that they are being used not served.

There is a concept in psychology and philosophy called "thin-slicing". Without going too far down the rabbit hole, it is the ability for people to draw accurate conclusions quickly from a disproportionately limited/small amount of data and/or interaction. What this means for you... people will "get it," and "get it" quickly.

Empowerment

How often have you received, and subsequently touted organizations that have provided quality service to friends, family, and co-workers? We marvel at organizations that are willing to step up, take responsibility and make things right.

In his book, *"Excellence Wins,"* co-founder and former CEO of the Ritz-Carlton Hotel Company, Horst Schulze, does an amazing job at relating how important, among other things, service is to the success of the Ritz-Carlton Company.

One of many examples involves empowering employees. At the end of a rigorous training and orientation period each employee is given a discretionary fund of $2,000 to be used by the employee to resolve any problem a guest of the hotel may have, no questions asked.

Understanding that the Ritz-Carlton Hotel Company is a very much for-profit organization, and that such a decision was made based on the profitability of loyalty relative to repeat business, the principle behind empowering employees is a sound one for any organization – including, most definitely, nonprofits.

Granted your nonprofit may not have $2,000 to give to each and every employee to use at their discretion but what are some things you can do to empower employees to assist them in caring for those they serve (remember, externally and internally)?

Let me give you a quick example. A nature preserve charges a day fee, let's say $15, to allow people who have not purchased an annual membership to gain access to their land, hike on their trails, etc., on any given day. One day a member shows up and has forgotten his membership card. Without proof of membership the member is asked by the fee collector to pay the

$15 day fee to gain access to the hiking trails. To make matters worse the member's family is accompanying him, all of whom have annual memberships and have forgotten their membership cards as well. As a result, the member is now asked to pay $60 for the family of four. Right or wrong?

There are those among us who would say "Right! Rules are rules. What's the point in having rules if you're not going to enforce them? If you make an exception for one, you'll wind up setting a precedent and have to make exceptions for everybody. Members should know the policy of having to show their membership card to gain access and if they forget it then that's on them." What do you think? On point or a bit too strong and narrow-minded?

In this case, I would have to go with a bit too strong and narrow-minded. How could empowering an employee in this case help? Yeah, I suspect it's pretty obvious. The fee collector now has the opportunity to help Dad look like a hero simply by letting them in without paying the fees – the coveted win-win scenario. In this example, the people were members, no materials, supplies, or resources are being consumed and I suspect that come membership renewal time you'll probably find a very eager person sending in their annual membership fee.

Studies have shown that people are not only more prone to turn into loyal, repeat customers but they are also willing to pay more for a product or service if they will receive quality customer service after the purchase is made. It is always more cost-effective to keep an existing customer than to have to go out and find a new one.

Of course, not all examples are as clean, cut, and dry as this one. Sometimes having a policy can actually help and protect an employee who might otherwise be put in a tough position regarding a decision to be made. The point is, has your organization intentionally considered the various circumstances, means, and methods by which you might be able to empower employees throughout the organization and by so doing give them a larger stake in the organization? If you have, kudos, if not you should probably consider doing so sooner rather than later.

Little Things

As discussed in the chapter, *K.I.S.S.*, contrary to popular belief small things can make a big difference. Things like truncating a value by .000127 in a weather prediction model, or French soldiers not having nails at the Battle of Waterloo, or, in my case, not having a piece of mail delivered one day earlier, all had substantial impacts on lives and/or the world as we know it.

Yet another example of small things making a big difference is the well-known One Degree Effect, or what experts in the aviation navigation arena call the 1 in 60 Rule. Simply stated, both rules affirm that at short distances being off one degree in the direction of travel has a minimal effect – at 100 yards you would be off by 5.2 feet. However, at greater distances the effect becomes substantially more noticeable – at one mile you would be off by 92.2 feet, and if you were traveling to the sun (although I have no idea why you would) you would be off by 1.6 million miles.

Of course, the arena of sports is notorious for examples of small, in terms of length or time, making a big difference. Take for example the 1,000-meter kayak singles at the 1988 Summer Olympics in Seoul, Korea – American, Greg Barton beat Australian Grant Davies by... .005 seconds or less than one centimeter. Or how about the 2008 Summer Olympics held in Beijing where Michael Phelps won the 100-meter butterfly by 4.7 millimeters (less than one-sixth of an inch). And there are still other examples of races won by an even smaller margin of victory.

In the world of politics there are examples of presidential elections being won by one vote. In the 1824 race between John Quincy Adams and Andrew Jackson, Adams won by one vote when it fell to the House of Representatives to determine the outcome. In the 1876 election between Rutherford B. Hayes and Samuel J. Tilden, Hayes won by one vote in the electoral college.

I could go on and on with examples of how "small" has shaped the very world we live in but I think you get the point... small things can make a big, sometimes huge, difference.

So, in terms of service, what small things can your organization implement that individually or cumulatively could have a noticeable and/or significant effect on those you serve? It might be something as simple as having a real live human being answering the telephone, or empowering employees to resolve customer complaints up to a certain level. Maybe it's posting pictures in online staff directories or organizational newsletters so that customers can put a face to a name. Truth be told there are probably dozens of small things you can do to begin separating yourself from the competition when it comes to service. Of course, each organization is different and so too should be your solutions. Just keep in mind it may not be anywhere near as difficult or costly as you think.

Remember, when things, even small things, come from the heart, when why you do what you do becomes evident, those you serve will know – and one of the added benefits... so will you.

CHAPTER 6

What? How? Why? Who?

There seems to be a prevailing wisdom today that says you are only as important as what you do, and subsequently asks the question, "What can you do to contribute to our success?" Of course, something deep inside us rebels at the notion but a quick survey of several organizations tells us, even more importantly shows us, that such a view is all too often accurate.

Unfortunately, such views are not confined to the workplace as evidenced by how quickly we've become a "disposable" society. Nowadays if something is broken (i.e. it doesn't do the "what" it was designed to do), we rarely take the time or effort to fix it, we just throw it away and get a new one. If the television breaks, get a new one. If we're having problems with a computer, throw it away and get a new one. If the refrigerator goes on the fritz, get a new one. If an employee is struggling, throw them away and get a new one. If anyone in one of the many relationships we are part of is not up to our desired standards, time to get rid of them and move on.

Even the sports world isn't immune to the effects of our disposable society. If you happen to be a fan and watch any of the mainstream sports (i.e. football, baseball, basketball, hockey) it has become standard practice that if a player isn't performing well, seldom will teams work at getting to the root cause of the underperformance and help the player improve. Instead, they get rid of the player and get a replacement.

I recently saw a post on a social media platform that illustrates the point all too well. A woman who had been married for seventy-five years was asked how she and her husband had managed such a feat. With a bit of sadness in her eyes as she reflected on the state of relationships today, she replied, "I grew up in a time when something was broken you fixed it, you didn't throw it away." – painful but true.

There is no question that many of the nonprofits that I've worked with have tended to be

laser-focused on what they do and how they do it –
their "what" and "how." At first glance it would
seem that such a focus is not only logical but
necessary, and in part that may be true – "in part"
and "may be."

When pressed on their "what" and "how"
most organizations tend to default to an almost
incredulous attitude that oozes, "Duh! Hello!
That's why we exist, to do what we do." After a bit
of back and forth, I'll clarify, "So you exist to do
what you do. Right?" With heads nodding
vigorously as if to say, "Stop stating the obvious
and get on with it," you can imagine the looks of
bewilderment when I respond, "Wrong!" With
heads shaking and feeling as though they were just
sucker-punched, it is a thing to behold, watching as
a sense of confusion sets in.

You see, for a variety of reasons I am a big
believer in the power of words. We all can relate
examples in our own lives when we witnessed the
power of words. How they had the power to build
up and the power to tear down; when they had the
power to heal and the power to destroy. Suffice it
to say, words are powerful. (I discuss this more in
the chapter, *Communication – A Lost Art*)

With this in mind, let's take another look at
the statement, "We exist to do what we do." The

truth is that what you do and how well you do it is incredibly important but it is <u>NOT</u> why you exist. Ready? What you do and how you do it are simply a means, a method, a way of fulfilling why you exist. The reason you exist is… to serve others.

Initially, it may seem like semantics, and maybe it is, but remember, words are important so let's take a quick look at the words. When you say, "We exist to do what WE do," the emphasis is clearly on you, the organization. But, when you shift the wording to, "We exist to serve OTHERS, and what we do is just a way of accomplishing that," the focus is now where it should be… on others.

The truth is "what" you do and "how" you do it are <u>internal</u> issues to the organization, involving programs, policies, processes, procedures, and other organizational resources. Unfortunately, when the focus shifts to the internal, many organizations become myopic, they develop tunnel vision with heads down and blinders on. They can quickly lose focus on what is going on around them and start ignoring the bigger picture. These organizations often adopt what can easily be misinterpreted as a somewhat arrogant, "This is what we do and how we do it – take it or leave it," attitude. The result... those being served begin to feel like an afterthought and not truly cared for. They quickly understand that the focus is more on the organization than on them.

Again, some might argue that it doesn't really matter as long as those being served get what they need, but as discussed in the previous chapter, *Service – It's a Matter of the Heart*, intention, why you do what you do, and remembering you exist to serve others, is incredibly important and will most definitely make an impression and have a significant impact on everyone concerned.

In stark contrast, "why" you do what you do and the "who's" you serve are externally focused. They lift our heads, take the blinders off and allow us to see what truly matters... those being served. Having an external focus allows an organization to see trends and circumstances that may have a direct impact on those being served and to respond appropriately and in a timely fashion. In the event something is amiss or not working to the benefit of those served, we can quickly make adjustments. But all of this can only be accomplished if we are intent on looking outwards.

One quick qualification/clarification that needs to be made at this point is the use of the term "external." As we'll discuss in the next chapter, *Who Do You Serve?*, some of those being served are internal to the organization and so when I speak of looking externally, those we serve internally are included. The point being, to get our focus off of organizational policies, procedures, and processes and consider the people being affected. Again, that's not to say that organizational issues such as policies, procedures, and processes aren't important, they are, it's just that they need to be in alignment with those being served.

As important as they are, when the "what" and the "how" get out of balance with the "why" and the "who," organizations, and the individuals that inhabit them, find themselves on a very slippery slope. It becomes easier and easier to focus on the "what" and the "how" and to start losing sight of "why" you're engaged in doing the "what" in the first place – the "who."

It can be like watching children grow. When you're with them day in and day out you don't notice the changes until one day you look at a picture that was taken five years earlier and the changes hit you like a ton of bricks. Similarly, organizations can wonder how they wandered so far from the organization they intended to be; how they became so internally and process focused, drifting away from the people they were created to serve.

It isn't easy for organizations to look in the mirror and acknowledge that they've made some poor decisions and wandered off the path, let alone to find the courage and the will to make a concerted effort to get back on track. It's hard but it can be done, and obviously the sooner the better.

Finally, I would be remiss to not reiterate that the ideas behind "what", "how", "why", and "who" apply to <u>all</u> those being served as discussed in the next chapter, *Who Do You Serve?* When an organization's employees (at any level) come to believe that they are only valued for the "what" – what they can do – and not who they are; that they are simply a cog in the organizational wheel and output is king, then I suspect you will find people who at best are giving minimal effort, and at worst teetering on the edge of leaving and looking to find a more compassionate employer.

As we've just briefly discussed, what people do and how well they do it is important BUT, and this is a very important "but", it should be the result of being valued not the reason to be valued. Being treated well, with caring and respect, will always manifest itself into a happier more efficient, more effective workforce, but remembering "why" you treat them well is all important – simply because you care and they matter. Amazingly, the rest will take care of itself.

Hopefully for most this will just be a slight adjustment, a relatively minor shift in perception but as with most things in this book it's the little things, and when you change the way you look at things, even the little things, the things you look at change!

CHAPTER 7

Who Do You Serve?

At first glance, it may seem like a silly question to ask anybody associated with a nonprofit let alone devote an entire chapter to it, but since it is at the heart of everything you do as an organization, I think it deserves some special attention. Besides, the very fact that I'm devoting an entire chapter to it should be a hint that there may be more to it than initially meets the eye. Remember, when you change the way you look at things... the things you look at change.

In the previous chapter, *What? How? Why? Who?,* we came to the sometimes-uncomfortable conclusion that you do not exist to do whatever it is your organization does, as amazing as that may be. You exist for one, overarching, all-encompassing reason... to serve others – what you do is simply a means to accomplish that. Of course, this begs one simple, fundamental question... who is it that you serve?

Since I'm clearly not going to let you off the hook without answering the question, most people will begrudgingly answer with the obvious – we exist to serve whatever constituency group we were created to serve. That can include anyone from the homeless, to the hungry, to an afterschool tutoring program, to abused women and children, to groups providing disaster relief services, to helping neglected and abused animals, to nature preserves, to hundreds of thousands of other amazing organizations. This all sounds well and good, and reasonable until I ask the next question – who else?

This is where the idea of changing the way you look at things becomes more relevant. Usually, folks will look at each other with a somewhat inquisitive expression on their face and then after some thought will come up with a great answer – we serve our employees. Great answer! Of course, given that this book is being written for everyone in the organization, a more universal answer might be, "Everybody serves everybody," or "We serve each other, regardless of position." Either way, you get the point.

"How do we serve each other?" you might ask – fair enough. Let's consider the following. To start with, the organization itself offers each and every person working for it the opportunity to make a living, to provide for themselves and their families. A healthy organization will also provide opportunities for every employee to utilize a specific skillset (hopefully based on a well-thought-out job description) that will provide meaning and fulfillment to their lives. The organization can also provide appropriate professional development opportunities to both improve existing skills and training to increase and expand an employee's current knowledge base.

On a more pragmatic level, employees provide reports and various types of other information to each other to assist recipients in the performance of their duties.

On a social level, employees provide each other with an avenue for social interaction. They can provide caring and a supportive ear when needed. Sometimes something as simple as a smile can help someone get through a difficult day.

You may not think it, but you serve your fellow employees more than you know.

At this point you may think that you have pretty much exhausted the various groups you serve but... you'd be wrong. Who else do you serve?

How about we ask the Development/ Fundraising people to chime in. I'm sure they have an inkling of who else you serve. If you said donors and/or potential donors you'd be right. Initially, you provide them with information about the effectiveness of your people and programs, what you do, and how you do it. Once they've chosen to support you, you provide feedback on how well you're doing, where their money is being spent, and how effectively it's being used. They might ask for things like financial statements or investment data if they've given to endowment.

You'll always make sure to thank them for their generosity and provide recognition when and where appropriate. And you always make sure to keep them updated on things that may be coming down the road such as projects, programs, capital needs, fundraisers, galas, etc., where you may be able to garner additional support.

In this category of those you serve, we'll also include granting agencies including Federal, State, and private foundations. Many, if not all of these grantors, will require some sort of reporting from you to ensure that you've abided by the requirements of the grant, and that's typically necessary to have your expenses reimbursed after the fact.

Are you ready? Who else?

How about volunteers? Don't you serve them? Here we're talking about those invaluable people who donate their precious time to help further your cause. If you don't serve them, if you don't provide appropriate opportunities for them to utilize their skills, if you don't take the time to recognize them for all the hard work and effort on your behalf, their commitment will be short-lived.

This category of those you serve also includes a very special category of volunteers – Board members. In addition to volunteering their time in a variety of ways, including committees, they typically provide financial support, networking, and outreach to spread the good news about who you are and what you do. They also provide expertise in areas directly addressed by your organization. In turn, the organization supplies them with a variety of information and reports so they can provide their governance and assistance more effectively.

Who else? I know, you're thinking to yourself, "You're kidding right?" Nope. Who else? How about contractors and vendors? You may be thinking, "Wait a minute... they serve us," true, but you serve them as well – remember you're changing the way you look at things. Just like an organization serves its employees by providing them with a livelihood, it also serves its vendors by doing the same. A vendor/contractor provides a service, just like an employee, and you pay them for it, like an employee. You provide them with the opportunity to use their specialized skills and if they're good you will provide them with additional customers via word-of-mouth referrals.

Who else? I know what you're thinking – "Come on! We must have exhausted the groups we serve," right? Not quite. Maybe you can think of others, maybe not, but there is one more group that I'll offer up for your consideration. This group will definitely get you looking at things differently and probably cause some eye-rolls in the process. Are you ready? The group is... everybody else. What?! Yeah, this is the one that typically gets the most exasperated looks and requires the biggest change in how you look at things, but hear me out.

When you consider those you serve you usually consider service in some form of direct interaction. There's a logical, definable exchange that occurs with a relatively obvious and noticeable outcome. However, there are also indirect consequences to every action, every exchange, every act of kindness you participate in – every life you touch will, in turn, touch other lives. Every life you affect will affect every life that life comes in contact with.

There is a wonderful short video circulating on social media that captures this idea beautifully. In it, an older woman states, "A society grows great when old men plant trees, the shade of which they know they will never sit in." What "trees" are you planting with your service? What seeds are you sowing, not knowing what they will eventually grow into?

We have all seen this phenomenon play out in our own lives, yet for some reason we seem to ignore it when it comes to how we see serving others.

I'm sure that you can think of things that happened in your life that led to other things, that led to other things, that led to other things, etc, etc, etc, that led you to where you are today. One thing leads to another, leads to another, and so on. Remove any one event, any one decision, any one act from the equation and things turn out completely different... it's called life.

Typically, we have no problem seeing this idea in action utilizing 20/20 hindsight, but what if you could embrace the possibilities before having to watch life play out? What if you acted now via the service you provide knowing, not hoping but knowing that it will make a difference down the road? What if you planted an acorn today, knowing that one day it would become a mighty oak? And the hard truth is that whether you think that way or not, whether you believe it or not, it will.

There is a story that a mentor and favorite author of mine, Andy Andrews, loves to tell his audiences that conveys the idea, and it involves a gentleman by the name of Norman Borlaug. "Who?" you may ask – Norman Borlaug. Don't be concerned if you don't know who Norman Borlaug is, most people don't. I didn't know who he was until I read about him in one of Andy Andrews' books.

You may be surprised to know that Norman Borlaug was awarded the Nobel Peace Prize in 1970 for his work involving the increase of the world's food supply by creating high-yield, disease-resistant hybrid corn and wheat that could be grown in areas previously unsuited for the crops. As a result of his efforts, Norman Borlaug is credited with saving the lives of over one billion – that's billion with a "b" – people from starvation and still counting. In addition to the Nobel Peace Prize, he also received the U. S. Presidential Medal of Freedom in 1977, along with numerous other prestigious awards. What's even more amazing, and applicable to our discussion, is how Norman Borlaug got into the position to accomplish what he did.

In the early 1840s Moses and Susan Carver purchased a small farm just outside Diamond, Missouri. Towards the end of the Civil War a group of Quantrill's Raiders attacked the Carver farm and kidnapped a servant woman and her child. After much effort by Susan Carver, they were able to make contact with the raiders and made plans to ransom the child that had been taken (there is no record of what happened to the child's mother).

Late one January night, at a lonely and isolated crossroads in Kansas, Moses Carver ransomed the child by giving the raiders his horse – the only horse he had – in return for a burlap sack that contained the child. Wrapping the child in his coat to keep him warm, Moses Carver walked all night and well into the next day back to his farm where he and his wife Susan would raise the child as their own – that child's name was George Washington, and he took the name of his adoptive family becoming... George Washington Carver.

The brilliant George Washington Carver eventually wound up at Iowa State University and at the age of 19 took a Dairy Sciences class. He was such a good student that his professor allowed his 6-year-old son to accompany George on his weekend botanical expeditions. As a result of his walks with George Washington Carver that 6-year-old boy developed a love for agriculture, eventually becoming Secretary of Agriculture under President Franklin Delano Roosevelt (FDR) from 1933 to 1940. That man's name... Henry Wallace. Then in 1940, Henry Wallace became FDR's Vice President. Acknowledging the vital importance of agriculture, and using his new-found power as Vice President, Wallace created a cooperative program in Mexico whose purpose was, among other things, to work on the development of hybridized, disease-resistant corn and wheat. The man hired to head the new program... Norman Borlaug.

We could continue going back in time to see how Moses and Susan Carver met and wound up in Diamond, Missouri, and back further still but I'm hoping the point is clear. Despite where you might see yourself and your organization on any particular timeline of events, there is no escaping the fact that those you serve and the service you provide can, and most likely will, have far-reaching consequences, consequences you may never see come to fruition.

Know that the lives you touch will most definitely touch others and the rippling effect of your kindness and generosity will plant seeds that one day will grow to become mighty oaks.

CHAPTER 8

Leadership – It's Probably Not What You Think

No discussion of any organization, including nonprofits, would be complete without some acknowledgment of the role of leadership and the correlation between leadership and the level of positive impact that organization has on those it serves.

Understanding that there have been volumes written on the subject, and many admired experts have made the topic the singular focus of their professional lives, I am not going to attempt any "in-depth" discussion of the issue in this brief chapter. Rather, what I hope to do is offer what I attempt to offer throughout the balance of this book – a different perspective.

Ironically, any discussion of what leadership is needs to start with what leadership isn't. My thirty-plus years of experience dealing with a wide variety of organizations tells me that most people when they hear the word "leadership" almost immediately think of senior management – those select boxes at the top of an organizational chart including such titles as CEO, CFO, COO, Executive Director, etc. To be clear, leadership has <u>nothing</u> to do with a position or job title – sorry, but it doesn't. Job titles simply define levels of authority NOT leadership. Authority and leadership are not synonymous – hopefully they coexist in those in authority, but I'm sure we can all relate experiences in our personal and professional lives when they didn't. We all know people with the title and authority who were/are awful leaders. Conversely, I'm sure we all know people with little to no authority who we'd follow anywhere. So of course this begs the question, "If leadership isn't about levels of authority or job titles then what is it?"

The sixth President of the United States, John Quincy Adams, has been often quoted as saying, "If your actions inspire others to dream more, learn more, do more and become more, you are a leader." John Maxwell, one of my mentors and a noted authority on the subject says, "A good leader is a person who takes a little more than his share of the blame and a little less than his share of the credit." Sheryl Sandberg, former Chief Operating Officer of Facebook, once said of leadership, "Leadership is about making others better as a result of your presence, and making sure that impact lasts in your absence." One of my favorite authors, Andy Andrews, says, "Great leadership is a product of great character." And still one of the greatest minds of our time, Albert Einstein, once said, "A leader is one who, out of the clutter brings simplicity... out of discord, harmony... and out of difficulty, opportunity." I could go on and on but I think the point is pretty clear, there is something else that makes leadership what it is, or at least should be.

Typically, when leading a discussion about leadership I will invite attendees to join me in a two-step exercise in an attempt to kick off the process of getting to the heart of real leadership – what I refer to as "authentic" leadership. When I say "authentic" I'm referring to the "real deal", the ideal, what leadership should be not necessarily what people have been subjected to throughout their personal and professional lives. Keep in mind the dictionary defines "authentic" as: "Not false or imitation: Real or actual" – works for me.

I'd now like to invite you, the reader, to join me in this very exercise.

Step One: Closing your eyes I'd like you to think of someone who, in your eyes, epitomizes what real leadership should be. They can be living or deceased, from any period in history. They can represent any discipline – for-profit business, nonprofits, government and politics, sports, education, law, religion, etc. The only requirement about who you choose is that in your mind they are the quintessential example of authentic leadership. Take fifteen to thirty seconds now.

Normally, most people find this first step surprisingly easy with a person or two just popping into their minds almost instantly.

Step Two: In this step, with the person from step one firmly in mind, close your eyes again and think of the traits or characteristics that make this person the ideal model of authentic leadership. Please, keep your answers to no more than three words – no biographies, just simple, to-the-point traits that made/make this person your perfect example of what an authentic leader should be. We will be completing one of two statements: 1) An authentic leader is _____, or 2) Authentic leadership is _____. Take thirty to sixty seconds now.

So far so good?

At this point I would usually ask the audience, one at a time, to start telling me what traits they came up with. Since that isn't possible here, I'll provide a list of the typical answers they provide in no particular order of importance (#'s 1 thru 20):

An authentic leader (is/has):

1. About others
2. Caring
3. Nurturing
4. Empowering
5. A good communicator
6. Inspirational
7. Visionary
8. Engaged
9. People-focused
10. Leads by example
11. Decisive
12. Confident
13. Integrity
14. Competent / Skilled
15. Trustworthy
16. Open-minded
17. Team builder
18. Responsible
19. Understanding
20. Grateful

In addition, I provide these additional traits:

21. Helper
22. Respectful
23. Concerned
24. Focused
25. Intentional
26. Possesses self-awareness
27. Action-oriented
28. Resourceful
29. Passionate
30. Possesses high EQ
31. Question asker
32. Supportive
33. Stimulating
34. Vulnerable / Honest
35. Life-long learner
36. Generous
37. Uses time wisely

38. Promotes "safety"
39. Prudent
40. Courageous
41. Purveyor of hope
42. Develops new
    leaders
43. Sense of humor
44. Humble
45. Consensus-seeker
46. Compassionate
47. Empathetic
48. Innovator
49. Believes in people
50. Energetic
51. Simplifier
52. Sees challenges
53. All-in / committed
54. Embraces change
55. Embraces failure
56. Forgiving
57. Mentor
58. Interested
59. Curious
60. Walks the walk
61. Genuine/authentic
62. Positive
63. Flexible
64. Resilient
65. Accountable
66. Perseverant
67. Problem-Solver

<u>Authentic leadership is</u>:

1. Many of the traits above
2. An honor/privilege
3. A trust
4. An obligation

Assuming that many of the traits you would have identified are on the first list, and possibly the additional list I provided, I then ask the all-important question: "Looking at the list of traits you provided, does anything strike you about the list in general?"

Typically, this question evokes some stares and questioning looks which miraculously disappear when I answer the question, but I'll give you another moment to consider the list, specifically traits # 1 through 20 above.

One more time, "Does anything regarding the list of traits strike you?" Ready? The vast majority of them (actually all but one) are "personal" – they speak more to who a person is rather than what they do. Not surprisingly this coincides perfectly with the quotes we looked at earlier in the chapter. Leadership is about who you are NOT what you do (i.e. not about a job title).

Again, with the list in mind, other questions present themselves: "Is there anyone who wouldn't want their spouse, partner, or significant other to have the identified traits – caring, nurturing, a good communicator, engaged, confident, integrity, trustworthy, about others, understanding, grateful? How about your children if you have them? What about family or friends? What about your co-workers? Is there any group of people you interact with that you don't think should possess these traits – not that they necessarily have them now, but should?" I suspect your answer is a resounding "No!", and that's exactly the point.

Clearly, the implications of such a mindset are obvious. The traits that make a leader a leader are not the purview of a select number of boxes at the top of some organizational chart and have nothing to do with a job title. They should be nurtured and embraced by everybody within the organization – from the most junior program associate to the Chairman of the Board and everybody in between.

The truth of the matter is that everybody is a leader. The only question is, are they a good one or a bad one? It follows then that it doesn't matter if an employee has any direct reports or is simply a department of one – John Maxwell, who I quoted earlier, once said, "The hardest person to lead is yourself." Yep, you can be a leader of one, however, the question remains, are you a good leader or a bad one?

Of course, no one person, no authentic leader possesses all seventy of the characteristics identified on the lists above (and I'm sure there are a number of traits that aren't on the lists). However, a study of success and the people who have achieved it, including successful (authentic) leaders, reveals that the vast majority of them possess a significant number of the traits to a greater or lesser degree.

The good news is that most people possess many of these traits already it's just that, like muscles that aren't used, they can atrophy, become weak, or even dormant. With that said, all of the traits mentioned are skills, skills that can be learned, improved, and/or rebuilt. Like anything else in life that's worthwhile it will take work – the only way to get better at something is to do it... practice. The only thing needed is an intentional desire to want to develop and get better at them.

So, what does all of this mean to you? It means you can get started working on them right here, right now. You don't have to wait for a Board resolution or permission from your boss. It's totally up to you. Remember, when it comes to becoming the best leader you can be, you are the "boss."

CHAPTER 9

Communication – A Lost Art

If you stop and take the time to look, you'll see that life is really about relationships, and nonprofits are no exception – they're all about relationships as well.

Since studies and relationship experts have proven beyond a shadow of a doubt that communication is a major and critical factor contributing to the health and well-being of any relationship, it becomes vitally important that we heed the warnings associated with the lack of quality communication, or as some would suggest, no communication at all (more on that later in the chapter).

On virtually every list identifying reasons for the failure of relationships, lack of or poor communication is typically listed in the top three, and often cited as the number one cause for the failure.

There is no doubt that in a world of information overload and nonstop noise, including email, texts, social media, soundbites, etc., where the average time to get someone's attention is approximately six to eight seconds, effective communication has become a critical skill all organizations must address and master to be successful at serving others.

Clearly, it would be impossible to cover such a massive topic in one short chapter – people have spent their entire lives dealing with, researching, studying, and writing about every aspect of communication and its impact on our lives. Instead, my focus will be on the various communication issues that I have both witnessed and had to deal with during my thirty-plus years of working with nonprofits. Towards the end of the chapter I'll also offer a "twist" on a couple of communication issues – because when you change the way you look at things, the things you look at change.

The dictionary defines communication as: "A process by which information is exchanged between individuals through a common system of symbols, signs, or behavior." Of course, this definition doesn't delineate between positive or negative, good or bad, or effective or ineffective communication but we will address that as we move forward.

One last issue before diving in. It is important to remember that a mere seven percent (7%) of communication has to do with the actual words we use. Surprisingly, things such as tone and inflection, body language, eye contact, facial expressions, and hand gestures account for a staggering ninety-three percent (93%) of what we communicate to others. This becomes even more important when we consider how much the average person uses methods such as texts and email to communicate, where we don't get a chance to take advantage of the nonverbal cues.

Trust

The first issue that needs to be addressed is the all-important matter of trust and the associated fear that ensues when trust is in short supply.

Stephen Covey, probably best known for his mega-bestseller, *7 Habits of Highly Effect People,* once said, "Trust is the glue of life. It's the most essential ingredient in effective communication. It's the foundational principle that holds all relationships together." – by no means overstated.

Unfortunately, the primary manifestation of trust issues seems to occur in employees who are afraid to give voice to their concerns for fear of retaliation, retribution, embarrassment, or being ignored. Of course, this begs the questions: Does your organization as a whole, and the various people within the organization, foster a healthy environment of open and honest communication? Can people speak their minds openly without fear of retribution and/or ridicule? Is everybody's "voice" valued? If the answer isn't a resounding "Yes" to all these questions then rest assured that communication is suffering dramatically and effective communication is all but nonexistent.

The problem I have witnessed more often than not when it comes to communication issues involving trust is that people on the higher end of the authority hierarchy (decision makers) believe that the organization fosters an open environment for communication, in contrast, people on the lower end of the hierarchy disagree. The result is that the disconnection is perpetuated, continuing in a downward spiral because those on the lower end of the hierarchy don't trust the process enough to let those on the higher end know about their feelings of disconnection.

Two more issues on trust that warrant a quick mention before moving on. First, trust is a two-way street. Typically, we think of trust in terms of somebody's trustworthiness – can they be trusted? But as with all things there is another side to the coin. The issue is not only can someone be trusted – to listen, to try to understand, to not assume, to not retaliate if a disagreement arises, etc. – but do they have the ability to trust others? Since communication is a two-way street, to be effective trust has to flow both ways.

Finally, on the topic of trust, there seems to be a long-standing practice among most people that trust is a commodity that must be earned, typically over an extended period of time. Here I have to part company with many of my contemporaries. I genuinely believe that right from the start complete trust should be given until the person receiving that trust gives the person conferring it a reason not to. From my perspective, trust isn't something you have to win or gain, it's something for you to lose.

Why waste months, sometimes years, working on developing trust in someone and miss out on all the advantages trust brings to the relationship? Of course you can get burned but waiting months or years doesn't preclude the possibility of getting burned anyway. The truth is if your hiring process works the way it should (a big "if") then initial trust shouldn't be an issue – after all, why would you hire someone you don't trust? Ernest Hemingway said it best, "The best way to find out if you can trust somebody is to trust them."

Listening

Aside from trust there is probably no other communication issue that elicits such a universally visceral reaction than "listening."

There are an alarming number of studies that have shown that the vast majority of people (90% to 95%) listen with the intent to respond NOT the intent to understand – which of course isn't listening at all. In other words, as someone is trying to communicate, the receiver is busy formulating a response rather than considering what is being said and attempting to incorporate the information being provided into their own understanding and response. The typical result is misunderstanding and/or a feeling of not being heard. Predictably people walk away from such an encounter feeling frustrated, confused, and wondering why they even bothered – communication begins to break down and relationships begin to fail.

Things such as being fully present, having a genuine interest in what the other person has to communicate, maintaining eye contact, patience, empathy, and noticing the non-verbal cues, are but a few of the skills that can be employed to improve the effectiveness of "listening." The good news is that listening is a skill that can be learned and/or improved. It takes a desire to want to get better at it and intentional effort but the benefits are well worth it.

Words/Jargon

Even though the words we use represent a small percentage of what we wind up communicating they can be incredibly important, and so it becomes essential that we choose our words wisely.

Using terminology and "jargon" that the receiver either doesn't understand or has a different understanding of can lead to ineffective communication at best, and frustration and total breakdown of communication at worst. Case in point: One of the nonprofits I worked with requested that I research and recommend a new telecommunications system for the organization. After doing some initial research I invited a couple of vendors to come into the office to make their presentations.

The first vendor brought four of their employees from various areas of their company to the table. After five minutes of listening to nonstop technical mumbo-jumbo, acronyms, system requirements, and telecommunications jargon, I stopped the meeting. I found myself needing to explain to the gathered "experts" that since I was the customer and that I would be responsible for defending the final choice of systems to senior management and the rest of the staff, I would need to understand what they wanted to do and why they wanted to do it. It was all well and good that they "got it", but if I didn't "get it" then we were just wasting each other's time. I am an absolute believer in Albert Einstein's quote, "If you can't explain it simply you don't know it well enough."

After another ten minutes of discussion that slowly degenerated into yet another "jargon-fest," to the surprise of those gathered, I ended the meeting. Ten days later I hosted another meeting with the same vendor's CEO who understood my concerns and did a great job explaining everything to my satisfaction. One week later they started installing the new system.

The point is that they came incredibly close to losing a substantial contract all because of "jargon". Just as the vendor in this example almost lost a substantial contract, you too can lose those you're trying to communicate with if, among other things, you don't choose your words carefully.

Lack of Feedback

A vital part of communication is "closing the loop," or getting feedback. Sending a message is one thing, but making sure the person, or persons, on the other end received the message and understood it as the sender intended is a totally different issue.

I can personally attest to the disconnect between what senders of communication believe they are communicating and what the intended receivers actually understood the communication to convey.

Again, the stumbling blocks can be the choice of words used, the communication platform utilized (i.e. verbal, texts, emails, periodicals such as newsletters, etc.), the message conveyed by nonverbal means, and/or the personal biases of both the sender and receivers, to name a few. The point is simply that in order to ensure effective communication the sender needs to lay assumptions aside and make sure that the message was both received and understood as intended.

Of course, there are a myriad of other issues affecting communication but hopefully, these thoughts are enough to start the dialog within your organization.

_____

As promised, here are two more thoughts about communication with a "twist."

There is a philosophical thought experiment that many have heard of that asks, "If a tree falls in a forest and no one is around to hear it, does it make a sound?" I would like to propose a similar question: "If someone speaks and there is no one there to hear it, does it constitute communication?" The answer is not only not as philosophical as you may think, it's actually more powerful and important than you may think.

To start with the answer is a most definite "Yes," but here's a twist... the sender of the message also becomes the receiver of the message. Truth be told this happens more often than you think. Not only does it happen all the time, but every single person in your organization participates in it – it's called self-talk.

You may scoff at the idea but time and time again science has revealed the power this type of communication has. Consider the following facts: your brain is <u>always</u> eavesdropping on everything you say; you have ten times more influence over yourself than external influences have over you; if the communication is negative, it's ten times more powerful than something positive; in the event you verbalize something negative the effectiveness is increased four to seven-fold – that means that negative thing you just verbalized is forty to seventy times more powerful than something positive. Still think self-talk is something to be scoffed at? You must always be conscious of, and extremely careful about, your "communications" when no one is around.

Finally, I am going to take exception with many of the experts who cite "lack" of communication as a major contributing factor in the failure of relationships. Although "lack" doesn't necessarily mean a complete and total absence of communication, in this context it implies a significant absence of it. Here's my problem, I don't believe that there is such a thing as "lack" when it comes to communication. I believe that we are always communicating all the time. The issue, therefore, isn't "lack" in general, it's the lack of <u>effective</u> communication.

Silence, which many would consider the quintessential example of a lack of communication, can communicate quite a bit if we take the time to look and understand what it's saying. It can be indicative of several things – fear (e.g. fear of retribution, retaliation, or embarrassment), apathy or indifference, and/or inappropriate ego issues that manifest themselves in feeling that there is no need to explain or communicate – to name a few. It can indicate a misguided sense of caring and not wanting to hurt the intended recipients – no one wants to be the bearer of bad or difficult news. It can indicate frustration or confusion. It can indicate anger on the would-be sender's part. It can indicate a lack of understanding of the need to communicate. Ultimately, it can even indicate a problem with the communication process in general.

You can probably come up with even more reasons for someone choosing not to communicate but the point is, you can't not communicate (sorry about the double negative).

Another important point about silence, or the absence of effective communication is that when communication is lacking people are left to fill in the blanks. Typically, most people will fill in those blanks by defaulting to negative reasoning – the communication isn't forthcoming because it's bad news, someone is mad or doesn't care. Whatever the reason, as we just talked about, what they come up with and the associated influence of how they choose to fill in the blanks is ten times more powerful on that person than what could have/should have been conveyed by someone else.

Finally, and I'll admit this is a personal peeve of mine, organizations should avoid "negative reporting" at all costs. Simply put, negative reporting says, "I'll only contact you if there's a problem," or "If you don't hear from me everything's fine." The problem is this – how does the person who would be receiving the communication know that they didn't get it because everything's fine OR things aren't fine and the communication got lost in the process, someone forgot to forward the message, or whatever communication system was being utilized had a problem?

Again, I understand that we could go wider and deeper on the subject of communication but hopefully the ideas and thoughts presented have triggered ideas and questions that will lead you to your own deeper consideration and understanding of the effectiveness of your own communication efforts and those of your organization.

Here's to changing the way we look at things!

CHAPTER 10

Comfort Kills

Nothing on this planet will kill dreams, ambition, desires, innovation, challenges, improvement, drive, determination, and excellence, faster and more completely than comfort. It affects organizations on every level and in its own way lulls them into a slow painful decline and eventually death. I know this may sound overly melodramatic to some but if you've ever witnessed watching people and organizations succumb to the addiction of comfort, all with a smile on their face, then you know how painful it can be. All ambition and dreams slowly and methodically drained from their being until their battle cry becomes nothing more than "Whatever," or "Good enough."

A few years ago, I saw a post on one of the few social media platforms I'm on, posted by a well-meaning person I'm sure, recommending ten resolutions to work on for the new year. For the most part I was on board with the first nine but the tenth one caught me completely off guard and had me wincing as if someone had taken their fingernails and run them across a blackboard. The tenth resolution? "Be comfortable." In my defense, I didn't reply to the post with some indignant, angry, hurtful response like so many people do, as a matter of fact I didn't reply at all, but it did get me thinking.

"Being comfortable," sounds all well and good, but is it really something we should be aspiring to? I don't think so. It can be a welcomed relief at times, and it would probably even be okay to seek out for its own sake on occasion, but something to aspire to as a constant condition of our lives? … definitely not.

Don't get me wrong, I know how wonderful it can feel to be comfortable, sort of like sleeping in on a cold winter morning, but I also know how vicious a master it can become if you let it. Keep in mind, I'm not talking about the comfort of finding that sometimes elusive operational flow when everything seems to be hitting on all cylinders, or that sigh of relief when some great challenge has been successfully overcome. I'm also not talking about the comfort found when a caring soul reaches out when you've suffered some great loss or the comfort of a sympathetic ear that listens when your world seems to have fallen apart and you don't know where to turn. I'm talking about comfort as a life choice, born of fear and a mediocre life, that settles for a comfortable "okay" instead of what can sometimes be an uncomfortable "amazing."

Author Neale Donald Walsch is credited with a quote that says, "Life begins at the end of your comfort zone." I don't know about life beginning at the end of your comfort zone, I've seen my fair share of unfortunate organizations and individuals existing quite comfortably within their comfort zones. What I do know is that a life full of energy, hope, joy, passion, purpose, and meaning can't exist very long within it, and will by necessity, burst through the comfort zone, out the other side and hopefully keep on going.

Comfort, your organizational brain's way of avoiding pain. In other chapters we've talked about how your brain, thinking it's your best friend and always wanting what it thinks is best for you, even if it's not, will tend to default to a few predictable patterns of behavior. However, this is so important that it bears repeating.

The first pattern – your brain loves what is familiar – for purposes of this discussion, "comfortable." Understand that "comfortable" in this context does not necessarily mean right, best, or even desirable, it simply means that your brain likes what it knows and is familiar with, be it good, bad, or indifferent. For example, say your organization has been less than effective in the delivery of its programming, to some degree your brain will fight to maintain the status quo, even when rationally you know it's time to change. Why? Because it's familiar. It knows what to expect even though it may be ineffective or inefficient, but it's a known. That's why breaking old habits is so difficult to do, they're familiar and your brain loves what's familiar.

Working in concert with the familiar, another way your brain will try to protect you, and to be clear, it's doing what it believes is in your best interest, is to move you away from pain and towards pleasure. Since change is usually perceived as "painful," and we've already acknowledged that comfort is your brain's way of avoiding pain, you can probably guess what happens – comfort will pretty much win out every time.

So, with the ideas of your brain loving what's familiar and wanting to keep you from pain in mind, enter the universal answer to both – comfort. As it turns out, especially in today's modern, western culture, not heroin, not cocaine, not alcohol, but comfort has become the drug of choice. What?????

Think about it, one of the dictionary definitions of a drug is, "something… that causes addiction, habituation, or a marked change in consciousness" – sounds about right. As a society we have become addicted to comfort in all its various shapes, sizes, colors, and forms, and as a result it can't help but find its way into the work environment. Isn't it true that the more comfortable you are the more comfortable you want to be? The more comfortable you are the harder it is to get up and get moving? The more comfortable you are the harder it is to change?

Everything from instant just about anything, to fast food everywhere, to drive-thru windows for just about anything, to credit cards so we don't have to experience the discomfort of waiting, to remote controls so we don't have to walk two feet to change a channel or turn the air conditioner down, to cell phones where we can text and not have to deal with the discomfort of having to actually talk to someone, to social media where we can filter everything about ourselves and not have to deal with the discomfort of who we really are, along with tons of other "conveniences" that help keep us comfortable, all help to tighten the stranglehold that comfort has on us. If you don't think so watch what happens the next time the batteries in the remote control go dead, or the next time the use of a credit card is declined, or a new manager is hired, or a policy is changed, or a major catastrophe happens like the internet going down, and you'll realize just how addicted we are. And the major challenge for organizations? Employees bring their reverence for comfort right into the workplace.

Like most drugs, comfort does its best to keep us in a state that we mistakenly interpret as being happy and content, when in reality it is uninspired, lethargic, ignorant, and always wanting its next "fix", and like most drugs, given enough time, comfort can, and will kill. As stated at the onset, it will kill dreams, hopes, aspirations, desires, passion, and in the most extreme cases has the capacity to even kill the body. Part of comfort's insidious nature is that it has the ability to permeate almost every aspect of our lives – mental, physical, spiritual, intellectual, and social. There's no area of our lives that is immune from its effects, and once it has gotten a foothold in one area of life it can spread like cancer.

Keeping in mind that we live in a dual universe, where everything has its opposite, we must constantly be aware that the very walls of strength, security, consistency, etc., we see as comfort providing – not allowing the difficult, uncomfortable, problematic things of life to get to us – can also turn out to be the walls of a self-imposed prison. Remember, walls not only keep the bad things from getting to us, they also keep the good things from getting to us as well. The very walls that hold the cruel, uncomfortable world at bay also hold us prisoner and prevent us from venturing out and experiencing the stuff that amazing lives and organizations are made of.

One of the major problems with comfort is that its lethargic effects lull us into a false sense of security. We've even developed trite, worn-out clichés such as, "If it ain't broke don't fix it," and "Don't rock the boat" to help justify the sedentary existence comfort provides. The truth is, if you want an organization that isn't mediocre at best, and wasted at worst, an organization that is more about fulfilling its mission with excellence than just getting by and existing, an organization that is more about embracing and savoring the opportunity to serve than just getting through the day, then my suggestion to you is... if it isn't broken, maybe it needs breaking. As far as rocking the boat is concerned, you have two choices, rock it, you'll be in great company with some of the best "boat rockers" of all time, or you can simply get out of the boat, it's probably filled with a bunch of lethargic sheep anyway. Isn't it great to have choices?

Eleanor Roosevelt once said that you should do one thing that scares you every day. It's also been said by many that are living lives of real passion, joy, and fulfillment that if your dreams don't scare you, if they don't make you uncomfortable, then you're probably not dreaming anywhere big enough. What's the point you ask? The point is simply this, service that makes a difference, service that matters, is usually lived well outside of comfort zones.

Not wanting to leave you with a sense of hopelessness, the question we now face is, "If comfort has us in its grips, how can we break free?" The answers are simple but not easy – awareness and action. Knowing that the issue exists is always the first step in solving any problem, and action is always necessary to make significant change. There's an axiom that states, "If you want something you've never had, you'll have to do something you've never done" – Ouch! I know, but there's no other way. Remember one of Einstein's famous quotes about the definition of insanity – doing the same thing the same way and expecting different results. You have to do things differently if you want things to be different, and trust me, your brain is not going to be a happy camper.

Here are some thoughts on staying away from, and out of the "comfort trap" (in no particular order). You'll note that many of them are mentioned in other chapters, however, they are all worth repeating.

First, be careful about lowering standards and expectations – with others and yourself. Initially, it may seem like you're just trying to be nice and understanding but the truth is once you start making compromises on the very things that are critical to your achieving the excellence we talked about in the chapter, *You Can't Give What You Don't Have,* you start down a slippery slope that at best is extremely difficult to recover from. Here's a quote credited to Michelangelo that may help, "The problem is not that we aim too high and miss the mark, the problem is that we aim too low and hit the mark."

For fans of SMART goals, I understand your concerns relative to the "A" – Achievable, but remember we're talking more about overall attitude than **S**pecific, **M**easurable, **A**chievable, **R**elevant, and **T**ime-bound goals. With that said, when implementing SMART goals make sure that people are being challenged especially when it comes to the "Achievable" measure – people will typically live up to, or down to expectations. Expect the best from people and most will rise to the occasion. Don't hold folks back by setting the bar too low – there is nothing noble or empowering about playing small and living below one's potential.

Another thought to help you stay away from the "comfort trap" is education – not in the sense of formal schooling and college degrees but rather a commitment to lifelong learning and improvement. Organizations need to make sure that there is a match between the position and the person filling that position relative to skill set. The easiest way to have people retreat to their comfort zones is to set them up for failure, after all, comfort zones are safe if nothing else. Invest, not spend (yes, there's a difference), in training and keeping skills relevant and up-to-date. A person confident in their skills and energized by their abilities is much more apt to step out of their comfort zone and embrace the challenges excellence requires.

Another idea that I have found to be invaluable when addressing comfort is to make sure that you are constantly assessing and reassessing skills, policies, procedures, and other matters that directly impact work performance. I think we can all agree that in today's world things are changing at breakneck speed. Things that may have worked and been appropriate six months ago, a month ago, or even yesterday aren't necessarily appropriate today. By reassessing things at appropriate and timely intervals, organizations can avoid becoming overly reactive which is usually a sign that they have become too comfortable with the way things used to be/always have been.

When I start working with a nonprofit I typically interview staff and ask a lot of questions. If, when I ask someone why they are doing something a particular way, they answer, "Because that's the way we've always done it," or "I don't know. That's what I was told to do," red flags pop up and bells and whistles start going off because I know a dangerous level of comfort has set in.

Due to space constraints I'll mention one more item, although there are many, before moving on, and that item is... Communication (for more on this topic see the chapter, *Communication – A Lost Art*). All too often people within an organization will fail to communicate effectively. People towards the top of the organizational hierarchy can either be demanding and impose their will on others, or not communicate at all because they don't feel they have to, or they don't want to "rock the boat." Any of these can be a sign of being too comfortable. On the other hand, people towards the bottom of the organizational hierarchy can find it difficult to communicate because they fear retribution for speaking out or ridicule for appearing unknowledgeable. In either case, they will retreat to their place of safety... their comfort zones. Overall, ineffective or poor communication within an organization can be a tell-tale sign that communication issues exist, and comfort may be at the root of the problem.

I could go on and on about all the various correlations between poor, ineffective communication and comfort zones but I think you get the point. By ensuring that communication channels stay positive and open, employees will be energized to share information vital to the achievement of excellence.

In closing, it is important to keep in mind that this issue, like most of the issues we've discussed, is not a matter of black and white – you're either comfortable or you're not – it's a matter of shades of gray. With that said the litmus test for whether you're too comfortable, or getting too comfortable, is a relatively easy one. Is the level of comfort you're experiencing inhibiting dreams, ambition, desires, innovation, willingness to accept challenges, communication, improvement, determination, and excellence? If so, then you need to acknowledge the issue quickly and determine to resolve it even quicker. Remember, comfort can and will kill... but only if you let it.

CHAPTER 11

The Power of Questions

There is a simple premise when it comes to questions – ask "bad" questions and you get "bad" answers, conversely, ask "good" questions and you get... "good" answers. This same idea harkens back to my old computer programming class in college when the favorite maxim circulating was, "Garbage in, garbage out." The hard truth is that we place way too much emphasis on answers and nowhere near enough value on the quality of the questions we are willing to ask. We do this at our own peril since we will inevitably follow where the questions we ask lead us. Ask inferior, poorly thought-out questions and you'll most likely waste a lot of valuable resources going down the wrong road.

Albert Einstein once wrote, *"If I had an hour to solve a problem and my life depended on the solution, I would spend the first fifty-five minutes determining the proper question to ask, for once I know the proper question, I could solve the problem in less than five minutes."* Pretty amazing coming from someone like Albert Einstein, but if you think about it, pretty much everything, including the world around us, begins, or began, with a question, more specifically, the right question.

It should be no surprise then that many, if not most, of today's top performance coaches, and organizational and leadership development experts, are all onboard with the idea that it is the quality of your questions that determines the quality of your answers, and in turn, the quality of your life as individuals, and as an organization.

As we've discussed previously, every great invention, every great movement, every great accomplishment known to man, has occurred on the other side of change. However, it should be noted that the impetus for that change typically had its origins somewhere in a question – "How can we do this particular thing better?" "Why do we allow such and such to happen?", "How do we do a better job serving those who are depending on us?", "How can we solve this problem?", "What would happen if…?", "Why do we keep experiencing this problem?", "Which opportunity is better for us?", "What should our priorities be, and why?", "Should we do this or do that?" – the list goes on and on, but the key is to understand that buried within the very questions we ask, lie the answers we seek.

Michael Beckwith, author, founder and spiritual director of the Agape International Spiritual Center, has said, *"Behind every problem there is a question; Behind every question there is an answer; Behind every answer there is an action. Behind every action there is a way of life."* Embedded in this philosophy is the understanding that at the very heart of problem-solving, for any problem your organization may face, lies an extremely simple and obvious question, "What is the problem?" That simple question followed by a series of subsequent, appropriate questions will lead to an answer – the right answer IF you ask the right questions.

There's an old adage that says, "When you don't know where you going, any road will take you there" – pretty profound if you think about it. The linchpin to the adage is knowing enough to ask the question "Where is it we want to go?" This is as true for organizations as it for the people they serve. Ultimately, it's one of the very questions that direct and drive our journey to the answers we seek.

Not surprisingly, the idea of asking the right questions permeates virtually everything we've discussed in this book. For example, in the chapter, *You Can't Give What You Don't Have*, we talked about the various ways to show caring for those we serve. One of the ways to make sure that those we serve feel valued and heard is to connect by asking questions – How are they doing? Do they have everything they need to be successful? Do they feel valued, and if not, why not? Do they feel as if what they do matters? Again, if not, why not? If they were in charge, what changes would they make and why? You may think you know the answers but care enough to ask.

In the chapter, *Communication – A Lost Art*, this very issue of listening appeared as one of the key elements to effective communication. Specifically, we discussed the critical difference between listening to respond, which studies show most people do, and listening to understand – listening to respond makes things about us where as listening to understand makes it about others.

Directly correlated to the idea of listening to understand is the proposition that one should strive to be more interested than interesting – again the focus on others (interested) versus the focus on self (interesting). The importance becomes clear when you consider that being interested in what others have to say must by necessity include listening to understand. And the connection to the topic of "questions?" In a vast number of cases, you show that you are truly interested by asking thoughtful questions.

In the chapter, *Leadership – It's Probably Not What You Think*, we identified being a "question asker" as one of the characteristics of authentic leadership. Strikingly, two of the chapter titles are themselves questions, *What? How? Why? Who?* and *Who Do You Serve?* I could go on and on but I think it's pretty clear that embedded in virtually every idea we've discussed lies an implicit, if not directly asked, question that begs an answer.

Ultimately, most organizations and their employees wind up being confronted with much deeper questions, questions that confront their very existence – "Are we fulfilling our mission? How do we know?" "What do the people we serve think we can do better?", "Are we doing what we should to keep up with the evolving/changing landscape?", "Are we challenging ourselves daily to be a better organization?", "Are we too comfortable?" "How are 'internal' relations? Do people feel engaged and heard?", "What one thing can we do better?", "What areas are we struggling in, and what can we do to improve them?", "Are there things we're doing that we need to let go?", "How have we grown/gotten better as an organization in the last six months?", "Are we where we should be?", "What one word would describe our organization?" On a more personal note, "What is it like to work with me?", "How am I affecting those around me?", "What would happen to the organization if I wasn't here?", "What skills do I need to improve sooner rather than later?", "Where do I see myself in three years? If not here, why?" Pretty heavy stuff, stuff a lot of organizations would rather not think about, but nevertheless stuff that's usually running underneath most of what's going on all the time. The fact that they choose not to acknowledge it, doesn't make it any less real or any less important.

I am an absolute believer that deep down inside, organizations, and the people that inhabit them, want to know that they matter, that what they do matters, that their existence has purpose and meaning, and that that meaning doesn't necessarily need to be created, it just needs to be found. I love the Mark Twain quote, *"The two most important days in your life are the day you're born and the day you find out why."* I honestly believe that there isn't an organization on the face of the planet that doesn't want to know in their inner most being that they're being successful in making a difference in the lives of those they serve

Simon Sinek, who in many ways has been a mentor of mine these past few years, has created what can best be described as a new awakening surrounding people, the businesses they populate, and the simple question "Why?" His best-selling book, "Start With Why," approaches the idea of purpose head on and gives substantial evidence that when companies, and the people they employ, focus on remembering "why" they exist, "why they do what they do," and when those "why's" are in alignment with basic core human values such as genuine caring, respect, empathy and service, then those organizations and their people, will tend to be more "successful" than those who don't know, or who have forgotten their "why."

"Why?" the simplest, most basic of questions, that somehow seems to miraculously coincide with a child's ability to speak. "Why is the sky blue?" (FYI, the common answer most people give about it relating to some kind of reflection off of blue water is completely bogus, but heck, what kind of position is a two-year old in to argue with you, right?) Anyway, if you've ever been a parent, or if you've ever been a child for that matter, and I assume most of you were children at some point, you'll have fond memories of the onslaught of questions, usually in response to being asked to do something – Please go take a bath... "Why?", Please, clean up your room – "Why?", Please stay close while we're walking through the mall – "Why?", Please stop asking me "Why?" all the time – "Why?" Yeah, fond memories.

One of the biggest problems we face each and every day is that through very systematic, methodical, controlling, and often deliberate actions, the various environments we operate within – well-meaning family and friends, not so well-meaning family and friends, the education system, employment systems, social systems, etc. – all conspire to subjugate our natural inclination to ask questions, and have all but drummed out of us any desire to question anything. As a natural byproduct of the cumulative effects of these environments we ask fewer and fewer questions, and become more comfortable and willing to accept whatever information is spoon fed to us. Okay, you caught me, I'm trying to soft-peddle this. The truth is we become lazy and complacent, taking the path of least resistance and the easy way out. We rely on so-called "experts", the internet, biased main stream media, social media, and a variety of other second and third-hand purveyors of information to tell us what we should do, how we should feel, and what we should think.

But here in lies a fatal trap – it becomes too easy to blame "the system" and become one of its victims. The truth is, as always, that the responsibility for what we think, how we think, or at the most basic level, that we think at all, is ours and ours alone – in many ways that's what this book is all about.

I totally get that asking the hard questions may lead us down roads to answers we'd much rather not get, and to truths we'd much rather not hear, but I would argue that a hard truth is infinitely better than a soft-peddled, well-dressed, diamond-encrusted, lie – and remember, a half-truth is just a lie in-training. If you ever hope to become the organization you were created to be, then you need the truths that can only come from asking the right questions, the hard questions. In the end we have the responsibility to ourselves, and those whose lives we touch, to ask the questions, sometimes hard questions, but in any case, as many questions as it takes to get to the truths we need to find.

One final thought/friendly word of warning. Beware of questions you are unwilling to ask and questions that you, or others, are unwilling to answer honestly – typically with answers such as, "Because," or "I don't have to answer to you," or "None of your business," or any one of a number of other defensive answers. Difficult questions are difficult for a reason and an unwillingness to address them honestly, or at all for that matter, is usually a tell-tale sign that they have struck a deep nerve that needs to be addressed before going any further since they will usually inform subsequent, important questions.

Let me end by leaving you with some questions: What are the questions you've been avoiding? Why have you been avoiding them? Are you afraid of the answers you might find? Do you think your organization, and the lives of those you serve, would benefit from you digging deep and searching for the answers to those questions? How would the answer to those questions change things? Powerful stuff, don't you think? Oh, one more question – what are you waiting for?

SUMMARY

So, there you have it – hopefully some ideas and a different perspective on some of the issues I've encountered along the way. As I mentioned in the *Introduction*, feel free to lay claim to anything you find useful and feel free to discard the rest.

In the first section of the book, *Method*, we discussed the two methods that create a lens through which the rest of the book should be viewed.

In the first chapter, *When You Change the Way You Look at Things...,* we talked about some of the objections that arise in your brain when trying to change – how it loves what's familiar and how it will always try to move you away from pain.

In Chapter 2, *K.I.S.S.*, we talked about the concepts of simple and our sometimes-misguided understanding of value relative to simple versus complex. We also touched on the impact and power of small. As examples, we looked at Edward Lorenz and the Butterfly Effect, the failure of French soldiers to carry nails at the Battle of

Waterloo, and the difference getting my ROTC scholarship one day earlier would have made.

In the second section of the book, *Application*, we applied the two tools developed in the first section, *Method*, to some of the issues facing nonprofits today.

In Chapter 3, *Change – Inevitable & Unavoidable*, we looked at the necessity of changing the way we look at change. We looked at the sheer magnitude of change that is constantly occurring and affecting virtually every aspect of our personal and organizational lives. And finally, we addressed the only two options open to organizations regarding change – ignoring it or embracing it.

In Chapter 4, *You Can't Give What You Don't Have*, we discussed the immutable law of the universe – that to give excellence to those we serve requires that we have excellence to give. We looked at ways to instill that excellence in our organizations by taking care of those within the organization first via mission/purpose, suitable skills, appropriate use of meetings, safety, and health and wellness to name a few.

In Chapter 5, *Service – It's a Matter of the Heart*, we looked at the importance of intention, and how the "why" behind what you do is as important, if not more important than "what" you do. We looked at an example (two different scenarios) of a wife awarded Manager of the Year and two different responses by husbands to their wife's news. We also talked about the importance of empowering employees if you want them to feel valued and truly put their heart and soul into servicing others.

In Chapter 6, *What? How? Why? Who?*, we talked about how nonprofits can become so laser-focused on what they do that they can quickly miss the point of why they're doing it. We talked about the sometimes-uncomfortable realization that nonprofits do NOT exist to do what they do – they exist for the sole reason of serving others.

In Chapter 7, *Who Do You Serve?*, we looked at what at first seemed like a pretty simple question to answer, but then again things aren't always what they appear to be. We saw that there are many different levels and types of people served, including "everybody else."

In Chapter 8, *Leadership – It's Probably Not What You Think*, we talked about leadership not having anything to do with position or job title. We did a two-part exercise to arrive at characteristics of "authentic"/real leadership and realized that authentic leadership applies to everyone in an organization, not just a select few at the top of an organizational chart. We looked at a list of seventy traits (feel free to add your own to the list) that authentic leaders possess to varying degrees.

In Chapter 9, *Communication – A Lost Art*, we discussed the importance of "effective" communication and discussed various issues that effect it including trust, listening, words/jargon, and lack of feedback. We also looked at the importance and power of self-talk. We also discussed the somewhat paradoxical idea that no communication or lack of communication can communicate a lot more than we think.

In Chapter 10, *Comfort Kills*, we talked about the detrimental effects comfort can have on dreams, ambition, desires, innovation, challenges, improvement, communication, drive, determination, and excellence. We discussed how "comfort" has become society's drug of choice. We reiterated the idea that your brain loves what's familiar, and familiar is comfortable. And finally, we touched on some ideas about how to avoid "the comfort trap."

Finally, in Chapter 11, *The Power of Questions*, we talked about the prevailing premise that the quality of the answers we seek is directly correlated to the quality of the questions we ask –

ask "bad" questions and we will inevitably get "bad answers, and usually waste a lot of valuable resources going down the wrong road as a result.

Of course, I probably could have written an entire book on each and every chapter, and maybe someday I'll do just that, but for now I just want to try to jump-start your thinking process, get you to consider alternatives, and look at things from a slightly different perspective remembering there are always two sides to every coin. In the end, nothing changes unless we do. Gandhi said it best when he said, "Be the change you want to see," and the best way to start the process is to change the way you look at things. Why? Because when you change the way you look at things... the things you look at change.

"Sometimes a change in perspective is all it takes to see the light." – Dan Brown

ACKNOWLEDGEMENTS

One of the most important lessons I've learned along the way is to always be grateful for pretty much everything but especially for people who have gone out of their way to help you. With that in mind, I have been truly blessed to cross paths with many amazing souls who have helped and provided sterling examples of what it means to serve.

My undying gratitude and thanks to my Mom and Dad who always showed me what it means to care about others. The lessons you taught and the examples you showed are forever ingrained in my heart and soul.

Thank you to Gail for your love, support, and editing expertise. It's been a long road but your support never wavered, truly a rock I can depend on.

Mentors are important and I have been blessed to have some of the best. A huge thank you to Nick and Megan Unsworth from Life on Fire. Your faith made it clear that choosing to work with you was the right thing to do. As promised, you over-delivered and made the process a lot easier than it would have been on my own. Many thanks to James Malinchak for your wisdom and ability to make what I thought would be difficult, easy, and simple. You more than lived up to your reputation of being the go-to person when it comes to crafting books that create business opportunities. I am indebted to Dr. Wayne Dyer. Thank you for your wisdom that will speak throughout the ages. You are missed. Thank you to one of my favorite authors Mr. Andy Andrews. Your ability to capture the imagination through your unparalleled storytelling continues to inspire me as I constantly reread your many wonderful books. Many thanks to Mr. John Maxwell who has inspired me throughout the years with his insight and genuine love for people and wanting to serve them.

Clearly, most of the ideas presented in this book were born in the crucible of decades of interactions with so many amazing nonprofits that are too many to mention. I thank God for each and every one of you and all the amazing work you do.

I'd also like to thank everyone who said "No," or told me it couldn't be done, and for all the people I've encountered along the way that showed me what not to do – they were hard lessons but invaluable lessons nonetheless.

To the hundreds of people who I've been privileged to meet along the way, who added their own "spice" to my life and I haven't mentioned specifically – thank you.

Finally, and most of all, I thank God for your tender mercies that are new every day – without you nothing would be possible. You are the quintessential example of what it means to serve others.

Scott Brown
June 2023

ABOUT THE AUTHOR

Scott's life has revolved around the ethos of service to others starting as far back as he can remember. It took a more definitive turn when he chose to serve his country by enlisting in the United States Air Force. Scott's distinguished civilian career began at IBM and then quickly transitioned to serving an assortment of nonprofits ranging from school districts to nature preserves to small nonprofit startups. Scott's expertise ranges from a wide variety of finance-related topics, including budgeting, financial reporting, general ledger, banking and investments, and payroll, to various administrative areas including policy and procedure development, risk management, human resources, benefits administration, and information technology.

Scott has presented at the Accountex USA national expo in Boston and has authored multiple books including *"I Think... NOT," "The Nothing"* (a fiction novel), and this book *"The Book on Nonprofits."*

Through his decades of executive service and experience with nonprofits, Scott has become a champion of the simple and all too often overlooked philosophy that merely changing the way we look at things can significantly impact the performance of an organization.

www.ScottWBrown.com

www.ingramcontent.com/pod-product-compliance
Lightning Source LLC
Chambersburg PA
CBHW070340220526
45467CB00001B/192